On Our Own
In Jerusalem's Old City

Two Born-Again Christians
Explore Their Hebraic Roots

Enjoy Jerusalem!

Vicki Andree

Vicki Andree

Aventine Press

On Our Own In Jerusalem's Old City
Copyright © 2010 by Dr. Victoria Andree

ISBN: 1-59330-633-4

Printed in the United States of America.

About The Covers

David photographed this meaningful stained glass window in Christ Church, the oldest Protestant church in the Old City. The stained glass portrays Romans 11:29-31 *"...for God's gifts and his call are irrevocable. Just as you who were at one time disobedient to God have now received mercy as a result of their disobedience, so they too have now become disobedient in order that they too may now receive mercy as a result of God's mercy to you."* "They, too," refers to the Jews. The olive tree represents Jews (menorah) and Christians (cross) in the same tree. See The Eleventh Day/Churches for more details.

The red heart-shaped string on the back cover was tied around my wrist at Rachel's Tomb (see the Fourteenth Day). David bought me the dress in the Muslim Quarter the day we walked the ramparts (see the Tenth Day).

Dedication

For David, my beshert.

My divinely appointed husband.

You bring out the best in me.

Acknowledgments

I thank my Lord and Savior, Yeshua HaMashiach. I dreamed of writing a book, but it couldn't be just a book. It had to come from Yeshua. This book discloses a tiny reflection of His generosity to me. "Delight yourself in the Lord and He will give you the desires of your heart" (Psalms 37:4).

This book would not have been possible without my husband David. Not only is he my hero and best friend, he spurs me on to things I think I could never accomplish. Besides moral support, he shares my love for Israel and especially the city of Jerusalem. His love for Yeshua comes to light in all phases of his life, which I love to watch. His patience, knowledge and persistence kept me going when I felt bogged down in the details. Thank you, David.

I would like to thank Daniel Segard for his excellent teaching. For over two years Daniel taught us Torah during Midrash on Shabbat. An excellent and knowledgeable instructor, you always put up with our 'weird' questions. Thank you, Daniel.

FOREWORD

What can I write about Jerusalem that hasn't already been written? Nothing. The only thing I could add to the volumes already written about Jerusalem is my own experience. So here is my story. Actually, it is our story. My husband, David, and I spent 26 days and 25 nights inside the ancient walls of the Jerusalem's Old City. Please join us on the adventure of a lifetime.

We experienced so many varied events each day that I faced the dilemma of how to title chapters. Because my brain operates sequentially, I settled upon numbering each day of our experience and noting one important site or teaching of the day. Since this solution made it impossible to list everything we did each day in the chapter title, the index provides additional references.

Strangely, until eleven years ago, I had no desire to visit the Holy Land. I love and follow Jesus Christ, our Lord, born in and raised in Israel. Yet, in my own mind, visiting Israel seemed *beyond the realm of possibility* for me. God speaks to me through my personal prayers and Bible reading. I never dreamed He would also speak to me through the Land. However, my God is a God of miracles. He has a way of making my dreams come true before I know they are my dreams. *"Delight yourself in the Lord and He will give you the desires of your heart"* (Psalms 37:4). God invited me to Israel on three completely different trips; once as a Bible student (1998), once on a standard tour (1999), and this last time on our own in Jerusalem's Old City (2009).

In 1998, my adult son, Craig Lockhart, invited me to join him in taking a course from Denver Seminary in partnership with Jerusalem

University College in Israel, *Geographical and Historical Settings of the Bible*. A required journey to Israel included in the course made it irresistible. The opportunity to study historical places of the Bible on site filled me with excitement! With some trepidation, I approached David with the idea of taking a college course requiring a trip. This meant leaving him alone for three weeks. His immediate response, "Yes, you should go," startled and elated me. Startled, because I last set foot in a classroom twenty-two years ago. Elated, because I was going to Israel! His enthusiastic and outstanding support during course preparation enabled me to excel. I owe him big time. The intense course work grew into a heartfelt challenge. In retrospect, the course marks a significant point in all of our lives. I warn you. Israel gets into your blood. The very next year I returned to Israel with David, my mother, and friends from our church for a tour. Since then, both David and I desired more time in the Old City – a least a week.

In the meantime, we began attending a different kind of Bible-believing church, a Messianic one! As we learned more and more about our Jewish heritage through Christ, our desire to return to Israel increased. A year ago we decided it was time. We picked a time of year and started praying and negotiating for a place to stay for three weeks in the Old City. With a Jewish and Christian calendar in hand, we laid out a schedule that grew to 25 nights. This included enough Shabbats and Jewish holidays, such as Lag B'Omer and Jerusalem Day, plus the Jewish Shavuot and the Christian Pentecost Days.

As soon as we booked our flights, Satan tried to discourage us. At a Fall Feasts conference, we heard Dennis Prager speak. He expected Iran to nuke Jerusalem in the spring. Should we wait? We prayed about it and decided no. It would be better to die in Jerusalem together if that should happen. Then the economy tanked. The trip would be expensive. Again we prayed about it. We could save money by eating only one meal out. The hotel supplied breakfast. We would take enough protein bars and shakes for at least one meal a day. Taking money out of the market at a low point makes it exceedingly expensive. We hoped to avoid that. David figured we had already lost far more than the trip would cost. Why not just go and enjoy the trip?

About this time, Satan attacked our health. David's knee acted up big time for the first time since orthopedic surgery over twenty years ago.

He kept re-injuring it. The MRI reported surgery wasn't necessary. He would need physical therapy at least twice a week. He is faithful to what he needs to do, but even up until almost the last week it remained a worry. Could he walk those cobblestone streets and steps of the Old City? He brought three canes, two knee braces, and tape. I injured my arm on New Year's Day. My own knee problems had been chronic for the last twenty years. My knees improved immensely since I decided to lose weight and concentrate on health issues. Sadly, they were flaring up again. In addition, my hip went out and I started having heart palpitations. We continued to pray. Over $3,000 of medical bills was a huge hit to the bank balance, but God kept saying we should go.

Now we praise God for His faithfulness and the gift of faith He gave us about this trip. Our desires included being able to relax in the Old City, something few tourists or residents have the opportunity to do. We wanted to take time to pray and respond at many different places, including places where people who live in the Old City pray. We wanted just a glimpse of what it is like to live in Jerusalem's Old City. This book is your invitation to join us in some of our many experiences in the city God claimed as His own. To God be the glory! He is greatly to be praised!

TABLE OF CONTENTS

Introduction

Kvetching in the Wilderness – Journey to the Holy Land

"…and in the morning you will see the glory of the Lord, because he has heard your grumbling…" (Exodus 16:7).

The airport shuttle drops us off at approximately 7:30 a.m. on May 6, 2009. The Delta agent checks our bags all the way to Tel Aviv. We won't have to deal with the four bags (totaling 200 pounds) at JFK in New York. Our carry-on luggage includes David's backpack and my forty-pound purse with computer. The flight to New York is pleasant. How could it not be? Delta provides us with personal TVs and snacks. The Lord furnishes good weather. I momentarily imagine how difficult travel used to be, centuries ago. Discarding that depressing thought, I push back in the soft leather seat, sigh deeply, and close my eyes.

We arrive at JFK thirty minutes early due to a 65-mph tail wind. The early arrival does us no good, though. The outgoing plane blocks our arrival gate, so we end up sitting on the tarmac waiting for our scheduled arrival! Anxiety sets in and I begin to get a little claustrophobic. Sometimes, not often, I get claustrophobic. Recently, I was stuck in an elevator by myself for forty minutes and I don't think I quite recovered. Thank Heaven this time I'm not alone. David sits next to me and encourages me to grip his hand. As you read the following pages, it will become obvious David is my hero. He's my good and perfect gift from God. Our love deepens and becomes more precious each year. Except when he works, we spend all our time together. A whole month with no work will be glorious.

David has been reading about Jerusalem for over a year now. He studied Biblical Hebrew before that, but it didn't stick. The past couple of months he revisited the Pemsleur (Quick and Simple) Modern Hebrew lessons 1-8 and then 9-20. These are by far the best conversational Hebrew lessons I have ever heard. Repetition teaches. Much repetition makes it fun to play games with the narrator. After listening several times, I start trying to say the phrases, before the narrator gets to them. I have fun with them. David is still working on lessons 20-30. We both listen to each lesson two or three times. It still doesn't always stick. In spite of that, the audio lessons help and our ear for Hebrew improves.

Once in the terminal, our four-hour layover at JFK flies by. David and I go directly to our gate and explore the area nearby. We read, people-watch (one of my favorite activities), and contemplate the eleven-hour flight to come. As the waiting area gradually fills with men in black suits, black top coats, black hats and curly long sideburns (called payos[1]), we realize many Orthodox Jews will be on our flight. It's fun to hear Hebrew in the JFK waiting room. Neither of us understands conversations, but occasionally words sound familiar.

Nearly an hour before our boarding time, the PA system announces everyone on our flight will be required to go through security again. A second security area awaits, complete with metal detectors and carry-on baggage x-ray machines between the waiting area and the aircraft. This comes as a bit of a surprise. I just started my first Hebrew conversation with a young woman sitting next to me when the announcement was made. "Sli-cha, at mevina englit?" *(Excuse me, do you understand English?)*

"Yes," she replies. The announcement blares over the PA system. Our group will be subject to the additional screening. We visit while waiting.

She is from Israel and has been visiting the United States for the past six months, mostly on the coasts. She mentions a news story reported Israeli security has gone lax. Israeli security dropped from the most reliable airport security to #4! David and I are shocked! Israeli security has always been the gold standard in world security. Now, America is zealous about security, too. As the herd of passengers obediently files past guards to a room off to the side, I can't help but notice the number of Orthodox Jews boarding. There are a lot on this flight. It occurs to me that over the centuries, Jews have been subject to special rules, rules much more demanding with much worse consequences than going through security checks a second time. Flashes of Hitler's death camps invade my mind.

The aircraft is full. We hunker down for the long flight. I'm disappointed because this older plane lacks personal TV screens. As close as the TV screens are, we are subject to the airline's movie choices. Some

---

1 The Old Testament says, "Do not cut the hair at the sides of your head or clip off the edges of your beard" (Leviticus 19:27). The word payos refers to sideburns or hair in front of the ears that extends below the cheekbones.

we've already seen; some we don't want to see. We listen to our iPods and language lessons. David listens to lessons 20-30. I'm on lesson 8. For some reason, I seem to pick up Hebrew faster. That's a joke. I had conversational Hebrew classes a couple of years ago. I didn't think I learned much then, but words come back to me now and then. I love the language.

Soon we will be in Jerusalem! They feed us after a couple of hours. To get into the spirit of this trip, we pre-ordered kosher meals. All the negative comments about airline food must be pure propaganda. These meals are delicious! One trip through the cabin after dinner and the crew disappears for the next eight hours. We sit next to business class and hear flight attendants busily pampering them. We smell their coffee all night long. Those of us in coach deal with things like hunger, thirst, and trying to get around people blocking the aisles. Whenever possible, Orthodox Jews pray standing rather than sitting. *"I stand in awe of your deeds, O Lord" (Habakkuk 3:2).* Their large black hats and long black coats with the beards and sideburn curls signify the traditional garb of a nineteenth century Jew. Many Jews in Israel today came from European countries. Sometimes, the dress suggests the country their country of origin. There are specific differences in the types of black garb worn for each Jewish sect[2]. The Orthodox Jewish men who dress like this set themselves apart from the conventional Jewish and the Gentile population.

Where are the flight attendants? Bathrooms are out of toilet paper. Disgusting! The crew evaporated. I want attention. I want snacks. I want to watch something else on TV. I want something to drink. I want to put my feet up. I just want to be there. *Me, me, me. Sometimes I get so sick of my own kvetching[3].* The Captain repeatedly asks the aisles to be cleared. He warns of turbulence often and instructs everyone to sit down and fasten their seat belts. Little turbulence actually occurs. The Orthodox Jews ignore him. Jews understand prayer is important. The "standing prayer (Amidah)[4]," which they say three times a day, must be prayed while standing.

---

2 There are three branches of Orthodox Judaism: Hassidic, Haredi, and Modern Orthodox.
3 Kvetch means to endlessly whine or complain.
4 The Amidah is the central part of all four services (shacharit – morning, mincha (afternoon), maariv (evening), and mussaf (additional). The word Amidah literally means standing because it is always said while standing.

Just before 9:00 a.m. Jerusalem time, the Orthodox Jews don tallit[5] and phylacteries[6] before beginning their morning prayers in earnest. There have been prayers throughout the flight, but when tallit and phylacteries come out, it inspires. God invites us to stop complaining and join the others praising Him. What an excellent idea. At any moment, in any situation, it is best to stop complaining and praise God. As Job reminds us, after he lost all his riches and his children, *"Naked I came from my mother's womb, and naked I will depart. The Lord gave and the Lord has taken away. May the name of the Lord be praised"* (Job 1:21).

The closer we get, the more we wake up, not that I ever actually slept. Anticipation invigorates us. Ninety minutes from Tel Aviv, the captain announces we are entering Israeli air space. He broadcasts that, according to Israeli law, everyone should be in his/her seat with seat belts fastened. In a much better mood now, David and I laugh. Think about it. Traveling at 600 mph, with a 90 mph tail wind, it will take us less than a minute to fly over Israel itself. Israel is 263 miles by 10 miles, about the size of New Jersey. It truly is funny! Israeli air space, indeed.

---

5 Jewish prayer shawls with tassels commanded by God. "Speak to the Israelites and say to them: 'Throughout the generations to come you are to make tassels on the corners of your garments, with a blue cord on each tassel. You will have these tassels to look at and so you will remember all the commandments of the LORD, that you may obey them and not prostitute yourselves by going after the lusts of your own hearts and eyes. Then you will remember to obey all my commands and will be consecrated to your God' " (Numbers 15:38-40).
6 Boxes containing Scriptures tied to the forehead and left arm commanded in Deuteronomy 6:4-8.

THE FIRST DAY

ARRIVALS

"By Faith Abraham, when called to go to a place he would later receive as his inheritance, obeyed and went, even though he did not know where he was going" (Hebrews 11:8).

Our flight lands two hours early. We brought more than the amount of food allowed for a normal visit. David confesses our transgression to the female guard at customs, expecting to pay import duty.

"Have any fresh fruits or vegetables?" she asks. David says we do not. She waves us through, "Enjoy your stay in Israel." We are in! We are actually in Israel. It doesn't feel like we are in Israel, but here we stand! We stand in the middle of a modern airport. Just to be in the Land feels surreal. One might ask, "Why would anyone want to go to Israel anyway? What's the big deal? Why do people hunger and thirst for Israel?" There can only be one reason. The God of the universe and everything in it, the Creator who created all things out of nothing, instructed Abraham to leave his country, his father's home, to go to a faraway land. Abraham, his wife, family, and possessions went to Shechem in the land of Canaan. *"The Lord appeared to Abram and said, 'To your offspring I will give this land'"* (Genesis 12:7). This land God chose for His people.

The God of Abraham, Isaac and Jacob, the God of Jews and Christians alike, spoke to Abraham. Consequently, Abraham came to the land in obedience to God. *"By faith he made his home in the promised land like a stranger in a foreign country; he lived in tents, as did Isaac and Jacob, who were heirs with him in the same promise"* (Hebrews 11:9).

The fathers of our faith homesteaded here, so to speak. God had a masterful plan to save a lost world. It's all coming down in this Land. God chose this place. That's what makes it the most interesting place in the world. It has a 3,500-year history recorded in the Bible, proven through archaeological findings and, even more important, through the life and death of His Son, named Jesus, or Yeshua in the Hebrew. In Hebrew the word yeshua means salvation. Yeshua, the most famous Jew ever, lived in

Israel. Being born-again believers in Jesus, we come to His Land. We come to feel closer to Christ and to walk where He walked. We come to pray in the holy places. We come to explore our Hebraic roots and to learn more about our position in the family of Christ. Galatians 3:29 says, *"If you belong to Christ, then you are Abraham's seed, and heirs according to the promise"*. As Abraham's seed, we have a lot in common with the Jewish people. Perhaps this journey will give us a better understanding of what that means.

We hire a sherut (minivan taxi) for the ride into Jerusalem. The mountains surrounding the city give me flashbacks to Old Testament battles and excursions. I imagine David accompanying the Ark of the Covenant into Jerusalem (II Samuel 6:16). I picture the Assyrian King Sennacherib's army surrounding Jerusalem where he bragged that he had hemmed Hezekiah in like a bird in a cage. The confident Sennacherib didn't fare so well and in the end God sent an angel to destroy the 185,000 soldiers waiting to attack Jerusalem (II Kings 19:35-36)!

I love the history. The smooth, wide, four-lane asphalt highway into Jerusalem is a far cry from what it meant when the Jews "went up to Jerusalem" to worship three times a year at the Temple. *"O Jerusalem, Jerusalem, you who kill the prophets and stone those sent to you, how often I have longed to gather your children together, as a hen gathers her chicks under her wings, but you were not willing"*(Matthew 23:37). Jesus made this declaration at His last contentious debate with the Pharisees in Jerusalem. Even though they plotted to destroy Him, he remembered His love for them. Many Biblical accounts race through my mind. It all happened here.

Our sherut stops on Mt. Scopus and Hebrew University before dropping us off just inside Jaffa Gate. The narrow street makes it impossible for the van to get us up to the door of the Gloria Hotel. We schlep[7] nearly 300 pounds of luggage about a block up the hill. These cobblestone streets are too narrow for normal traffic. Sometimes a small vehicle can get through, but even pedestrians must move carefully between short stone pillars, bicycles, carts, etc.

The entrance to the Gloria Hotel changed since our visit in 1998. I approve of the renovations. Back then I entered a simple black wrought iron door just off the narrow street and climbed a long set of marble steps

---

7 Schlep, whose derivation is Yiddish, means to carry clumsily or move about laboriously.

before getting to the one elevator. The elevator serviced only one floor. I remember climbing those steps from floor two to floor three back when I was here eleven years ago (the 1998 trip). There were days I didn't think I could take another step after being out on ancient sites all day. My arthritic knees hate stairs.

The Gloria Hotel's new lobby.

Now a lovely courtyard and ground floor reception area greet us. We check in just before a large tour group arrives. David notes the difference between our Delta crew and the Gloria staff is "as different as night and day." Our bags beat us up to our room. Oh, that bed looks so good. I fight off the urge to crawl in it immediately and fall into blissful sleep. Over 24 hours ago, we left Denver. We need to stay awake as long as possible. If we stay awake now, we might sleep through the night and hopefully recover from jet lag. We drag ourselves to the dining room where a full buffet awaits!

Our room consists of twin beds, two nightstands, a desk, a dresser, 12-foot ceilings, and a painting over the beds depicting David Street with an opium smoker in the foreground. The storage closet contains shelves on one side, which we fill with our snacks, protein bars, powdered drinks, vitamin supplements, and medicine for a month. The other side affords a small hanging space. We hang a total of seven shirts. Our private bathroom reflects 1940s modern decor. The bathtub plug doesn't work very well. Outside our sliding glass door a lovely courtyard beckons. An ornate water fountain completes the beautiful flowered patio. Doves come to drink and bathe. Our son, Craig, would be so impressed with the new entrance to the Gloria with all the little areas for sitting and talking. Now three elevators go from G to 3!

After dinner, we take soda baths recommended to combat jet lag. The hotel staff brings ice for David's hurting knee. We use the 220 volt heating pads a friend gave us. They are wonderful! Aches and pains melt away. Praise the Lord!

The Second Day

Grafted In

"If some of the branches have been broken off, and you, though a wild olive shoot, have been grafted in among the others and now share in the nourishing sap from the olive root, do not boast over those branches. If you do, consider this: You do not support the root, but the root supports you" (Romans 11:17-18).

Morning comes early. The Muslim call to prayer at 4:00 a.m. doesn't bother me. I'm wide awake. The soda bath apparently didn't take. I fall asleep again from 5:00 to 8:30 a.m. David wakes me for breakfast. The Gloria breakfast buffet (served from 6:30 to 9:00 a.m.) looks exactly the same as it did eleven years ago when Craig and I stayed here. I brought instant coffee for a reason. The water (even bottled) tastes awful! I'm using stevia and lime to make it possible to drink. By the end of the week, I'm sure I'll be used to it, but for now – ugh! Anything, such as coffee, made with this water also tastes awful. David drinks the tap water plain, but notices it never entirely quenches his thirst.

After breakfast we decide to explore. Instead of heading down to Jaffa Gate and David Street, we turn uphill into new and unfamiliar territory for me. Always the adventurer, David leads the way. The narrow, cobblestone streets curve in and out, up and down, with hardly any people in sight. A right turn puts us on Casa Nova Road. It's more like a wide, long staircase than a street.

The Women's Alliance Shop catches our attention. We peek in. This shop, run by West Bank women, sells items made by West Bank women (clothes, scarves, etc.). Because many of the West Bank men do not work, the women are *liberated* and must take charge to make some money. It is easy to see this may have a profound effect on Muslim culture in the future. The interesting part of our conversation with the women clerks is about the Pope's upcoming visit. They think it unimaginable either Arabs or Christians would want to harm the Pope. One woman mentions they will be closed Tuesday because of the Pope's visit. She says many secret service agents and security have interviewed them. David says, "They do that because they don't want any trouble."

One of the women laughs, "If there's trouble, it *won't* be the Palestinians or the Christians; it *will* be the Jews!" That makes me sad. The pro-Christian and anti-Semitic contrast surprises us. More than that, it shocks us! Uncomfortable with the conversation, we move on.

I reflect on the conversation. As Christians, we are joint heirs with Christ and He is our Brother. Christ is Jewish and that makes us part of a Jewish family. Romans chapter 11, gives a good explanation of how this works. Verse 17 reveals how God grafted us into His family, *"...some of the branches have been broken off, and you, though a wild olive shoot, have been grafted in among the others and now share in the nourishing sap from the olive root..."* Our response is that we love the Jewish people. How can we not? They now are family by the graciousness of God and the sacrifice of Christ. Unfortunately, those Christian Palestinian women don't seem to have the same understanding of these Scriptures as we do. Since Jews are God's chosen people, we should love them and certainly respect them. I am in awe of the Jews.

Christians often forget, or perhaps never understand, that Jews remained Jews after they accepted Jesus as the Messiah. All of the disciples were Jewish. After Jesus ascended into Heaven, Peter and John went up to the Temple at the time of prayer. Jesus never told them to discontinue that particular practice (See Acts, chapter 3). He never told them to stop being Jews. Acts 5:13 reveals that believers used to meet in Solomon's Colonnade, which was part of the Temple. Paul and the disciples preached the message of Jesus from the Temple courts. The New Testament, with the exception of Luke and Acts, was written by Jews. The Lord taught me for many years before I began to understand my relationship with the Jewish people. Being grafted in, I am like an adopted child.

In 1899 Mark Twain wrote about the Jews.

> *"If the statistics are correct, the Jews represent merely one percent of humanity — an irrelevant spark in the light of the Milky Way. Normally speaking, the Jews should hardly be heard of, and yet we hear of them again and again. They can rival any people on earth in fame, and their significance in economy and trade are in no ratio*

to their population. Their contribution to the list of great names in literature, natural science, art, music, finance, medicine and profound learning is just as amazing. They have done extremely well in the world – with their hands tied behind their backs. They could rightly be proud of themselves. The Egyptians, Babylonians, and Persians came into power, filled the earth with their glory, but perished. The Greeks and Romans followed, 'made a lot of noise,' and then disappeared. The Jews saw it all. They beat them all, and are today what they always were, showing no decay, no aging, no weakening, no decline of energy, no blunting of their wide-awake dynamic spirit. Everything is mortal except the Jew. All other powers perish but he remains. What is the mystery of his immortality?"

Continuing down this street, we encounter a hardware store in the Old City. It carries lots of merchandise for locals. We need a stopper for the bath tub. The package of sink stoppers includes two stoppers. The clerk opens it and sells us one stopper. The service is practical. We only need one stopper and he still has one in stock. In the United States, we would have had to buy the whole package. Outside, his friend smokes the traditional water pipe. Picturesque, yet not touristy because the hardware store caters to locals.

Intrigued by the delivery system to local shops, David takes pictures. A van parks on the narrow street. The van becomes a distribution center. Beer and Pepsi are lugged up to the liquor store on the stair-street we just came down. Boxes of electronics go by handcart to another store. And another cart takes boxes of other merchandise for yet another store. These carts that get pushed uphill or downhill are ingenious. The simple unexpected and fun braking system fascinates David. Strong teen aged boys push the cart uphill. For downhill runs, an old tire chained to the cart dragging on the ground becomes the brake. The boy guides the cart in its free fall downhill. He places his foot with enough weight on the old tire to slow it down just a bit. At times he has one foot on the tire and one foot on the pavement, like a skateboarder. Other times, he has all his weight on the tire slowing it down as much as possible. This system works especially well in this hilly city.

When a local cat hears the cart, he hides. Cats abound here. People like cats because they keep the pests down. However, no one I know here actually owns a cat. People feed cats to keep them alive. Many times, walking back to the Gloria, I see dried cat food sprinkled along the edge of the street.

Not far down the same street we venture into a shop where a man works on something at the end of the narrow room. Turns out, he makes jewelry and sells all kinds of merchandise. David Joseph Fatho, a friendly Christian Palestinian, owns this shop located in the Christian Quarter. He shows us a variety of things. Each item involves a story. He happily recounts each one. We find Jerusalem crosses and many unusual items. Every time we start to leave, we find something else to look at. We spend a couple of hours here and only the two Davids know how much money. Shops take both dollars and shekels, so it gets confusing. The shekel equals about 25¢ at this time. We leave the shop and wander down this fairly quiet street. It circles back to the Gloria. Now we have tasted the Old City of Jerusalem on our own. Like chocolate, I find Jerusalem delicious and addictive.

Some snacks, a little nap, and straightaway we find ourselves back on the streets of the Old City. This time, a very aggressive little man nearly drags us into his *new* shop. The shop, located in the back room of a street front jewelry store, didn't look new to me. It features carpets. It takes some time, but we finally convince him and the two men already here we aren't interested in investing in carpet. They immediately usher us into the jewelry store. Using every high pressure, low pressure, good guy, bad guy tactic I've ever heard (I have a background in sales), their efforts succeed. They manage to sell us an Iranian (to support the Jews in Iran, hm-m-m, very suspicious) tablecloth with a Hebrew blessing on it, some jewelry, and a gift the little man gave me. The gift, a white scarf, he ended up charging David 100 NIS (New Israeli Shekel)! This leaves a bad taste in David's mouth. We got good merchandise and, after half an hour of games, a decent price. After bargaining in the souk (a market in an Arab country) like tourists, we anxiously move on to real experiences.

The highlight of the day happens at the beginning of Shabbat (Erev Shabbat). Shabbat begins on Friday evening, usually with a special meal. Erev[8] is the Hebrew word for evening. Erev Shabbat means Friday evening. Shabbat lasts one full day, until sunset Saturday evening. We want to do

8 The Jewish day is measured from evening to evening because in Genesis, chapter 1 God says, "And there was evening and there was morning – the first day." Jewish holidays begin on the evening of the previous day.

something special to commemorate this day. We decide to journey to the Western Wall.

David on the steps down to the Western Wall.

A little history about the Western Wall might be in order here. In 70 AD, when the Roman General Titus destroyed Jerusalem and the Second (Herod's) Temple on the Temple Mount, only the retaining walls remained standing. The Western Wall, which resides closest to the Holy of Holies, became the holiest of Jewish sites. Jews testify God remains within the mountain behind the Western Wall in a special way. Many Jews come to pray at the Western Wall throughout the week, but especially on Friday evenings. Jews gather at the Kotel Plaza next to the Western Wall on holidays. Often, Bar-Mitzvot[9] and other celebrations take place at the Western Wall. People write prayers, fold them into tiny squares, and place them in cracks in the wall. The Kotel Tunnel Tour information on aish. com explains the tradition of placing notes in the Western Wall like this:

> *There was a Sephardic rabbi named Rabbi Azulai, who originally came from Morocco. When he was a young man, he left his teacher —*

---

9 Mitzvot is plural for Mitzvah. The word comes from the root word tzavta, which means connection. There are 613 mitzvot.

his teacher was the Ohr HaChaim, who was a master of Kabbalah — and his teacher said: "Okay, you're going to Eretz Yisrael, the Land of Israel, and what I'd like you to do — I'm going to give you a little note — I want you to put that note into the Western Wall."

In those days, when they would travel, they would not carry things like valises as much as we would today. Something that's really important, in order not to lose it, they would actually sew it into their clothing. That's exactly what he did — he took this note and sewed it into his jacket. Surely enough, when he got into Eretz Yisrael, he forgot about the note. It just slipped his mind. He got involved in his life, and for a long period of time, things weren't going so great. He was new here — you know the old expression, "Everyone's uncle here in Jerusalem is a rabbi — we don't need another rabbi." It's not an easy profession here in Jerusalem.

So he was having a hard time. But then when he was down, he realized that he forgot about his teacher's note! He went to that old jacket of his, he opened it up, and he found the note. He took the note, and he brought it down to the Western Wall, and put it into the wall.

The next day, he was sitting in the Beit Midrash, in the synagogue, and someone came over to him and asked him a question in Jewish law. It happened to be the particular part he was reading that day. He knew the answer on the spot. A series of events happened which seemed like luck, but it's too coincidental to think that it's just by chance. His fortune, his situation, changed, and soon he was recognized for who he really was — a great scholar and saint. Until then, he hadn't been the kind to push himself forward, and he never got the recognition he really deserved.

The Rav of the community noticed the change, and he said: "Something's really strange here. Up until now, I happened to admire this Rabbi Azulai, but it just seems strange that all of a sudden his fortune changed." So he came over to him and he asked him, "Come on, tell me — what happened? Was there anything that happened that changed your fortune? Did you do anything spectacular? Anything special?" Rabbi Azulai said, "Nothing really."

He kept hammering on, and pressuring him, so finally Rav Azulai said, "Yes, actually, my teacher gave me this note to put into the Wall, and I recently placed this note into the Wall."

So the Rabbi of the community begged him to go down to the Western Wall and see what the note said, because he knew the note was from his teacher. Rav Azulai said, "Okay, fine. We'll go down and take a look." So they looked and found the note, and opened it, and it said: "Dear G-d, please let my student, Azulai, become successful in the Land of Israel."

So that's the story. That's the tradition that we have. The idea is not that we're praying to the wall, and not that there's any sort of superstition, but rather because it's so clear that there's a Divine Presence here, that even writing a prayer on a piece of paper is like praying. It's like a continual prayer for that particular person, for that particular need.[10]

In observance of the requirement to dress modestly at holy sites, I wear a black skirt and top with my new black scarf. David wears his white shirt and black pants with suspenders. We look like a Jewish couple, and we are, grafted in. From the Gloria, we hike to the Western Wall. You go down David Street, jog a little to the left to the Street of Chains, then – the Western Wall. Many stairs occupy these *streets*, which are really bazaars. Watching our steps makes it difficult to peek into shops and walk at the same time. Any slowing down or delay causes merchants to appear and pressure you to come into their store. We want to get to the Wall rather than shop. We keep our heads down most of the time. When we get there, security checks our bags. We pass through the metal detector. David sets it off. Even after emptying his pockets, his knee brace sets off the metal detectors. Once through security, we descend the long, wide stone stairway onto the plaza. Lots of people face the famous Holy Wall.

---

10 By permission from the article "When did Jews start putting notes in the Wall?" Aish.com Webmaster www.aish.com

One approaches the Wall with reverence. A dividing wall separates men from women.[11] Because of this, David and I split up. I lose sight of him. I wash my hands in the cold water at the cleansing fountain (later I find out the ritual is to rinse each hand three times with the plastic cups in the fountains). I advance slowly in measured steps to the women's side. The space at the bottom of the Wall shades a crowd of praying women. Most of them hold their prayer book (siddur) as they pray. Determined to get near the Wall, I wait until I spot an opening. I slip in between two women. My determination comes with dual purpose. We are here to worship our Lord. I have notes with prayers I have promised people back home I will pray and place in the Wall. I brought my book of Jewish blessings and prayers. I pray the Amidah (standing prayer), reading in Hebrew. After thanking Him profusely for this experience and opportunity, I pray promised prayers and place tiny, folded notes into cracks between the large stones. I reverently bow and carefully walk backward away from the wall until I back into a wooden podium! Startled, I leap back to reality. I turn, seeing David in the distance where we agreed to meet.

David went to the men's side of the wall. He spent fifteen minutes in deep prayer standing next to the Wall. Because of chronic back pain, he rarely prays or even sings while standing. He prayed for many things. He praised God and thanked Him for His many blessings, including me. He also brought prayers to place in the wall. He prayed in tongues a lot and added his quiet murmurings to the overall prayers in many languages, including Hebrew prayers. Shabbat at the Wall consists of many languages intermingled praising God. A man and his four-year old son sang family Shabbat songs next to him. On the other side, an Orthodox Jew davened[12] and prayed. David felt the power of these prayers. Praise the Lord!

Up the stairs and on the Street of Chains, while carefully watching the intermittent steps and cobblestones, I hear an Orthodox Jew joyfully cry out, "Shabbat Shalom!" My head is faced down watching the steps. I wave and answer "Shabbat Shalom!" Too bad he can't see the big smile on my face.

---

11 In Orthodox Jewish shuls (synagogues), men and woman do not worship together. One explanation offered is that women and men are very different, in their thought processes, emotional states, and psychology. Prayer is supposed to be a time to be your true self. Orthodox Jews believe that men and women need space from each other to help them become in tuned to their higher selves.

12 Daven means to recite Jewish liturgical prayers, to sway or rock slightly.

Dinner beckons from a place called "Friends" on the Street of Chains. The salad bar includes a fluorescent pink colored cauliflower and grilled chicken on a skewer. The chicken tastes delicious. Once inside, the restaurant looks surprisingly large. Dimly lit, the Jerusalem stone walls soak up any light from the street. However, the cauliflower on our plates reflects off our faces! Four people sit at the only other table in use. We welcome the quiet atmosphere and share with each other our personal prayer times at the Wall. God's presence overwhelmed us when we touched the Wall and prayed.

The Pope is coming to Jerusalem. On Tuesday, he will come by our little street, right past the Gloria. Perhaps we will get a look at the man. Who knows? I love being in Jerusalem. We walk back to the Gloria past shops and busy merchants. Our busy day begins winding down. Almost there, a familiar face pops out and asks if we would like to see his new shop.

The Third Day

The Chosen People

"For you are a people holy to the Lord your God. The Lord your God has chosen you out of all the peoples on the face of the earth to be his people, his treasured possession" (Deuteronomy 7:6).

Our third day in Jerusalem begins with the same hotel breakfast. Our dining room view provides entertainment. We watch a cat walk the ramparts, then a single tourist followed by a large group of tourists. Yes, this little window on the world provides great entertainment every morning. I enjoy it immensely because I love to watch people. Right now I feel privileged.

After breakfast, we take a trip back in time. I show David the rooftop room Craig and I shared in 1998 when we attended our class at Jerusalem University College. That started it. Since then, I haven't been able to think of going anywhere but Israel, especially Jerusalem. We can see the rooftop rooms from our courtyard. It looks like the hotel added these few rooms onto the roof as an afterthought. Going up to see it again brings back good memories. We creep out onto the roof from room 301. What a spectacular sight! Up until now, David has taken all the pictures. Today, I get my camera out. The citadel, ramparts, shops, churches, the King David Hotel across the way and the famous YMCA building stand out as worthy candidates. I aim the lens and start shooting. From the rooftop we see laundry hanging in many places, reminding us people live in the old city. Sometimes we forget the residents because of all the shops, offices, and churches.

I spend the afternoon resting, reading, and writing while David goes exploring. Tomorrow we go to the Kotel (Western Wall) for the Tunnel Tour and the Chain of Generations Tour. I'm resting in anticipation of the strenuous day to come. I also catch up on emails and call home to let them know we arrived safely.

David goes exploring alone and farther than intended. His knee survives. Praise the Lord! First he goes to the Tourist Information Center around the corner. He wants to get a map. He checks out the access to the Ramparts Walk we can see from our breakfast table. He also checks on when the citadel (David's Tower) will be open and when the Night Spectacular shows. He runs into our pushy salesman friend at Jaffa Gate - the one who gave me a shawl, then charged David $25 for it. David's sense of humor kicks in and he asks the man if he could take his picture.

Later, David gets tricked into entering another shop. This time he buys nothing. He resists the sales pressure and repeats "no." Afterward, he walks the road to Zion Gate and around the Jewish Quarter. He intends to explore the Armenian Quarter, misses his turn, and doesn't realize it until he gets to the Jewish residential parking lot. He examines the bullet holes in the walls by Zion Gate. He watches two cars squeeze through the gate by a busload of tourists looking at the bullet holes with their guide. He recognizes the language as French from his college days and figures out the gist of what the guide says from his previous knowledge of Zion Gate. David turns to go back to the Gloria, when a new friend named Joseph tells him the Ramban Synagogue is open on Shabbat (today), so he should go visit. It turns out David's new *friend* is a licensed tour guide, so he ends up paying for this helpful information. It does give him courage to don his kippa[13] and go in to pray. A Midrash[14] in Hebrew in front of the room absorbs the Jewish men. David prays for fifteen minutes in the back without bothering anyone. The Midrash reminds him of our congregation back home.

Our congregation back home, firmly dedicated to the teachings of the Jewish people and our own Hebraic roots, recognizes the Jews as God's chosen people. We agree whole-heartedly; the Jewish people remain God's chosen people. That fact has not changed over the centuries, even though many times the Jewish people have turned from God. This truth testifies to the faithfulness of God. Jews remain God's chosen people. They have not been replaced by Christians.

The replacement theology taught in some arenas embraces faulty doctrine. God never intended for Christians to take the place of Jews. Christians become His chosen people only by being grafted in. The indisputable Word of God reveals this certainty in Romans 11:19, *"You will*

---

13 Also known as a yarmulke, a skullcap worn by Orthodox or Conservative Jewish men.
14 Midrash is a Hebrew word that means interpretation. It can refer to a specific way of reading and interpreting a biblical verse.

say then, 'branches were broken off so that I could be grafted in.' Granted. But they were broken off because of unbelief, and you stand by faith. Do not be arrogant, but be afraid. For if God did not spare the natural branches, he will not spare you either." Christians should not think themselves superior because God rejected some Jews. Abraham, the revered father of both Jewish and Christian faiths, has faith which looks like the root of a productive olive tree. The Jewish people make up the natural branches of the tree. Secular Jews account for the broken branches. Like a wild olive shoot, the Bible says, we are grafted in. Now, both Jews and Gentiles share the nourishment of the tree, based on faith. Deuteronomy 14:2 reconfirms what God said about Jews earlier, *"For you are a people holy to the Lord your God. Out of all the peoples on the face of the earth, the Lord has chosen you to be his treasured possession."*

$3,000,000 solid gold menorah in the background awaits the new Temple.

As David sits in this synagogue, surrounded by God's chosen people, he prays. *Lord, it's David, again. Your power and kindness amaze me. Thank You so much for allowing me to meet You in this special place. I am comfortable here. I feel Your peace. Thank You for sending Joseph to direct me here to meet with You. Thank You so much for my beautiful wife. She rescued me from the swamp of self-centered delusion and lured me into Your light. I am forever grateful for Your gift of the perfect wife for me. What a perfect helpmate she is. She completes this broken man. I don't deserve her, but as You know, I would be lost without her. Bless You, Lord, for You have blessed me.*

Father, thank you for these men here who love You and faithfully study Your Word on the Sabbath. Please bless the young man who is enthusiastically teaching now. Anoint him and give him Your Word and understanding to encourage his class. There are fewer men here that I would have expected in the middle of the Jewish Quarter. Bless Your faithful remnant. Please increase his minyan[15] that they might glorify Your Name.

I intercede for each of them for their personal needs, their concerns over jobs, health, friends, and family. Bless them, O Lord, and hear their prayers. Be the refreshing cool water that restores their souls and gives hope. Please strengthen the young man on the aisle who seems to need Your touch. For my own family I ask . . . Thank You for Your blessed Son. In His Name, Amen.

He listens for a few minutes to the Midrash. He catches a few words of Hebrew, but not many. They talk about prophets, which means, they study the Haftorah[16] section today. Jews understand better than anyone in the world that the highest form of worship is the study of God's Word. Their worldwide methodical study of Torah sections, week after week, year after year, is a testament to their faithfulness. Afterward, David heads back to the Gloria. Desiring to avoid David Street, the souk with its slow-going steps, he tries the "rooftop promenade" mentioned on his map. He ascends the stairs to the roof and wanders around on this local shortcut. Broken furniture and trash indicate the scarcity of tourist traffic. Soon, he asks an armed teen guarding a Jewish Yeshiva[17] the way down. He descends past the Yeshiva in session, down very steep stairs into a backwater street in the Muslim Quarter. David heads as fast as possible back toward the

---

15 Minyan is defined as the minimum quorum required for communal Jewish prayer. In Orthodox Judaism, ten males constitute a Minyan.
16 Haftorah is a short selection from the Prophets read on every Sabbath in Jewish synagogues.
17 Yeshiva is an institute of higher learning where Jews study primarily the Talmud. It also refers to a Jewish elementary or secondary school with a curriculum that includes religion, cultural, and general education.

central area and gets reoriented on his map.

David soon reaches Murad's messianic jewelry store (www.jerusalem-christian-jewelry.com). He goes in to discuss the tallit clip he wants them to make for him to match the silver scroll pendant he plans to buy me. After they choose the design, Murad graciously leads David back to the Gloria via the shortest route. Hopefully, he won't get lost again. David's been gone all afternoon. I'm glad to see his sweet face.

After a little rest, we go out to see the city at night. The lights shining on the walls of the Old City make it look like pure gold, which of course, spiritually speaking, IT IS! The New Jerusalem will shine like gold with the light of our Lord, Yeshua! We meander around Jaffa Gate and find some great little pubs. We speculate that Craig and his friends hung out here back in 1998, while I was recovering from days on archaeological sites. Oh, yes, I do remember the pain I endured during those wonderful first days in Israel. Thankfully, that is not the only unforgettable thing.

I want to stay up late tonight in hopes I will be able to sleep all night. We play our favorite card game, Hand and Foot Canasta. David beats me unmercifully one game. I guess he's allowed to win sometimes. At 10:30 p.m. we retire. I enjoyed this quiet day.

THE FOURTH DAY

THE TUNNEL TOUR

"The chief leader of the Levites was Eleazar son of Aaron, the priest. He was appointed over those who were responsible for the care of the sanctuary" (Numbers 3:32).

I slept all night! Hooray! Jet lag gives way to happiness and feeling human again. Breakfast is the usual. Today, the coffee tastes like real coffee at home. I am adapting, and that is good. We truly are amazing creatures. Only God could have designed such resilient capabilities in us. A three-day recovery heralds a personal best for jet lag from Colorado.

Craig's fortieth birthday reminds me to email a birthday greeting. Scott, our oldest son, and his wife, Gina, visit Seattle today to celebrate with Craig and his wife, Renee. They sleep soundly now, but in a few hours they will be getting up early to get a look at us at the Western Wall. Technology allows us all to share Craig's birthday and Mother's Day, even though we vacation half a world away. After our Tunnel Tour, we plan for prayers at the Western Wall. David alerted Craig when to log onto the live feed on Wallcam at aish.com.

David planned quite a schedule for today. Months ago, he reserved our spots today for the Chain of Generations exhibit and Tunnel Tours at the Kotel. He agrees it develops into much more of an adventure than he imagined. After breakfast, we write post cards. We wrote ten on Friday and ten today. Getting post cards written and mailed make this morning's agenda. Our friends and family may receive them before we get home. I prepared for this by printing off mailing labels before we left. David is not the only planner in this family.

Before starting out on our adventures today, we take pictures of our lovely courtyard. A beautiful day: cool but sunny, with just a little breeze makes the courtyard inviting. The fountain and flowers provide the perfect place for pictures. David sets the camera, taking pictures of the two of us together. An adventure like this requires numerous pictures. I use my digital camera as a photo journal. You know what they say, "a picture is worth a thousand words."

A little after 11:00 a.m. we start our walk to the Kotel. A friend reveals a secret way around David Street, helping us avoid a lot of steps, crowds, and pushy vendors. We begin at Jaffa Gate, go up the hill past the post office, and stick our noses in the Christian Bookstore. It looks inviting and I'm sure we will go back. I'm glad it's so close.

We take a sharp left and venture through some narrow, residential back streets. Names like St. James Street, El Aram Street, Ararat Street pass by. Soon we come to the Cardo Plaza. Back home I have been reading *The Streets of Jerusalem,* by Ronald L. Eisenberg. Every street name involves a story. St. James Street, even though very narrow and steep, is described as a "major street of the Armenian Quarter of Jerusalem, where the Cathedral of St. James is located, built on the site of the tombs of two figures in Christianity who shared the same name – St. James the Apostle and St. James, the brother of Jesus." El Aram amounts to a tiny street that didn't make the book. Ararat Street brings to mind "the mountain where Noah's ark came to rest" (Genesis 8:4). Tradition relates this site to Mount Ararat, the highest peak (about 16,000 feet) in the easternmost part of Turkey, adjacent to the Armenian Border."[18] Since reading the book, street names inspire history lessons. However, I digress.

We remember the Cardo as a special place. Mom and David sat in this very place back in 1999. We dropped out of the tour for a day to spend time with Mom in the Old City. She had a difficult time keeping up with the tour. We wanted to slow down, too. Tours usually take their toll on the mind and body. We ended up in this spot in front of Cardo Pizza. I remember David sitting here and enjoying pizza with Mom so I could trek over to the Wall. It's a good memory for us since Mom passed away two years ago. The Cardo Pizza shop still serves, so what else could we do? In Mom's honor, we order a slice of the best pizza in town! We toast Mom with our sodas and share a good memory of her doing something fun with us. Her good heart lingers in our memories and inspires us to love more deeply and forgive more quickly.

David carries my purse, filled with my coat, snacks, and stuff I always take. He doesn't mind carrying the bag; however, the short straps don't

18 Reprinted from *The Streets of Jerusalem* with permission of Devora Publishing.

fit his broad shoulders. We check out a few shops looking for a Bedouin bag. In and out of shop after shop, but no one has the perfect bag. Every shop carries a myriad of merchandise. We want to go everywhere and do everything, but it doesn't have to be today. We must pace ourselves.

We pass Hurva Square near Ramban Synagogue where David prayed yesterday. He knows the entire history of the Hurva (ruins) Synagogue's original destruction. The political battle on rebuilding styles kept it from being rebuilt after the Six-Day War in 1967. Teddy Kollek accomplished a great deal of renovation during his many years as mayor. Kollek had one arch constructed as a temporary measure until he achieved the final compromise. He believed the reconstruction would begin in a few years. Eventually, the arch became a landmark and there was no acceptable plan in sight. Kollek's vision finally came to fruition. Now it is being rebuilt. It pleases us to know progress continues. The original was never completed – thus the name Hurva (ruins). Even though the rebuilt one suffered destruction by the Jordanians, this symbol of Jewish presence perseveres. Modern architecture encapsulates an interior like the building the Jordanians destroyed, creating a great symbol of Jerusalem, old juxtapositioned with new. Even buildings highly honor traditions and the chain of generations. The price paid by previous generations persists in the Jewish mind. The subject of our upcoming tour covers all this and more.

The show starts in a few minutes. We hustle through a slow security check line (impossible) to make it on time. By some miracle, we make it right on time. The Jewish *Chain of Generations* begins with an inspiring movie of a candle representing Abraham. Candles increase as the generations pass. Abraham's descendants become as numerous as the stars. What an inspiring picture of God's promise, fulfilled. As we review the adversities the Jewish people suffered, the tour turns heart wrenching. Soon, my sadness gives way to exhilaration. Exhilaration because in spite of everything they still exist! This emotional trip through time told through glass sculptures and special lighting amazes me. Music with narrative adds to the wonder. Beginning with Abraham and Sarah, the story continues to present day Jewish families. Jerusalem plays the part of the golden thread tying it all together. The glass sculptures represent the generations of Jews. Viewing the exhibit in this place, so near the Wall, deeply moves everyone. We wish we could understand and read Hebrew fluently, but English audio tells the story well. At the end the memorial wall lists names of soldiers who died fighting for Jerusalem. It breaks our hearts. We owe them a great debt. It is humbling to be part of this heritage. The fact that Jews exist today can only be attributed to the Lord God Almighty who made Heaven and Earth. We must never forget the graciousness of God, Who made it possible for us to be grafted in to His chosen people.

David touches the names of fallen soldiers.

Leaving the *Chain of Generations* tour, we take a different set of steps up and out of the Kotel. With three hours to kill before the Tunnel Tour, we go exploring. Up new stairs, we find a building marked "Food For Needy." Right next to it a building titled BAR MITZVAH catches our attention. David's back is killing him after all the standing at the *Generations* exhibit. I'm ready for a break, too. We rest in chairs outside BAR MITZVAH for a time. We are looking for a snack. They seemed to be serving some kind of brunch. I sit on a bench near a man watching some children play. I take pictures of the cute youngsters. An elderly man says something in Hebrew I don't understand. He smiles. I smile back. A realization begins to creep over me. This gathering celebrates someone's Bar Mitzvah! We've crashed someone's party. We leave before the Bar Mitzvah party returns from the Wall.

Around the corner, up more stairs and to the right, we run into the Dan Family Building Aish School, aish.com – the Wallcam! I am excited! How many times have we logged on to aish.com looking at the live feed of the Western Wall? A few feet from the entrance we sit on a shady stone and eat our snack. People go in and out of the Dan Family Building. Four or five bicycles sit outside the door. We are surrounded by *long* stone stairways! I can't help but wonder at this. Soon, a student leaves, collects his bike, and carries it up the stairs.

Curiosity leads us into a shop where we meet a trained Torah[19] Scribe. He writes the small scrolls Jews put inside the mezuzahs they place on their doorposts. The Scriptural basis for mezuzahs found in the Book of Deuteronomy says. *"Write them on the doorframes of your houses and on your gates"*(Deuteronomy 6:9). *"Write them on the doorframes of your houses and on your gates, so that your days and the days of your children may be many in the land that the Lord swore to give your forefathers, as many as the days that the heavens are above the earth"*(Deuteronomy 11:20-21). The Scribe writes with a quill (feather) and ink on specially prepared animal skin almost like leather, called parchment. He also writes names for tourists in Hebrew on parchment. We want a mezuzah[20] with one of his parchments inside. Try as we might, we can't find a mezuzah we both like in this store.

Moshe and Dov Kempinski, shopkeepers Craig and I met in 1998, still run their shop, Shorashim. In 1999, when I brought David to Jerusalem, I made a point to introduce him to them. These men took time to teach us about Israel and the Jewish faith. Several people from our congregation visited Moshe and Dov's shop over the years. Moshe and Dov enjoy a reputation among people who visit their shop as men who willingly discuss things of God. They help in many ways. As Christians, we found them

19 The Torah represents the first five books of the Old Testament comprised of Genesis, Exodus, Leviticus, Numbers, and Deuteronomy. Their Hebrew names, in order, are Bereshit, Shemot, Bemidbar, Vayikra, Devarim. Each Torah is completely hand written, without error. It takes a trained Torah scribe an entire year to create a Torah scroll.

20 Along with the biblical passage from Deuteronomy, the word Shaddai (a name of the Almighty) is inscribed. Observant Jews affix a mezuzah to the doorframes of their homes as a sign of their faith.

especially helpful in broadening our understanding of Israel and the Jewish people. I wonder if they know how famous they are.

We take pictures along the way and end up in front of their shop, hoping to find the Bedouin bag and mezuzah. I visit with Dov about last time we saw him. He laughs, "Is it all right if I say I remember you?" We all laugh. I can't even guess how many tourists, students, and pilgrims he spoke with since we saw him ten years ago! I enjoy our conversation, but unfortunately they don't have the bag for which we search. We desperately want to buy our mezuzah from their shop, but only find a *maybe* in lovely dark brown leather. We look around some more. Out on the streets we come across a unique silver door to an apartment building. David poses for a picture. The door swings open and an Orthodox Jew emerges, dressed in black, carrying a briefcase. It must be difficult living in the Old City and putting up with the tourists.

A few more shops and around the corner we find a huge bookstore full of mezuzahs! The Moriah Book Store offers a profusion of books, scarves, mezuzahs, and more. After some looking, we find the perfect mezuzah. David finds a journal. I get a little notebook for our outings. I plan on coming back here soon.

The very best part of the Moriah Book Store experience is a 15-month old little Jewish boy named Eleazar. His Orthodox Jewish abba (Hebrew for father) stands watching him in the stroller as I sit under a shade tree outside the store. Eleazar smiles a big grin. "Hi," I smile back. Then, "Oops! I mean Shalom." Previous interactions with Orthodox Jewish men indicate that they do not chat with Gentile women.

This man in the Orthodox Jewish black coat and hat replies in a friendly American accent, "He knows how to say hi." We chat. God gives us a demonstration outside the book store that you cannot judge a book by its cover, or an Orthodox Jew by his coat! We enjoy a great conversation. He and his wife and child come from New York. The toddler got to come because he could sit on their laps. His older brother required his own ticket, so he stayed with grandparents. This toddler's smile outshines the golden lion statues next to the bench!

I ask if I can take his picture. I make sure I only take Eleazar's picture, so as not to take advantage of the father's graciousness. In my heart, I ponder the name Eleazar, a famous name carrying great significance. Aaron, the first high priest of Israel, named one of his four sons Eleazar. Eleazar became the chief leader of the Levites. He took responsibility for the care of the sanctuary in his early service. Later, Eleazar became high priest. The alternate spelling, Eliezer, refers to Abraham's faithful servant who probably secured Isaac's bride. Moses named his son Eliezer to carry on the honorable name. Many other fathers did the same. His name saturates the Torah. What a darling child. *Lord, bless this beautiful child. Grant him faith that he might love and serve You, just as Eliezer loved and served Abraham. Amayne..*

Nearly time for the Tunnel Tour, the line for the security check winds all the way up the stairway. Our turn arrives. Since the x-ray machine quit earlier, security manually checks bags. When David goes through the metal detector, bells go off frantically. He digs out of his pocket change and pulls out a small pen knife with a 1 1/2 inch blade. One guard immediately picks up the penknife, opens it, and holds it high over our heads to show the other security guard. At the same time, the other guard opens the bag from Moriah's Bookstore and spots the mezuzah.

"You Jewish?" he asks David. Then, I guess he decides only Jews buy mezuzahs. He waves us out onto the plaza steps before we can answer. With that, we get to the Tunnel Tour ten minutes early.

The Tunnel Tour includes more than when we visited in 1999. It demands no less than an hour and half of walking, standing, and stairs. New discoveries happen daily. This tunnel surely qualifies as an archaeologist's dream. There are more arches, more mikvahs[21], more relics, more ancient walls, more, more, more of everything to be uncovered! Honestly, I don't see how they can keep expanding the tour before splitting it into several tours, like the Hearst Castle in California did with their tours.

Our tour guide is a young woman well versed on the subject. She genuinely impresses me. She relates personal stories connecting her family to the Wall, making the tour fascinating. Her grandmother survived the holocaust. Knowing her roots gave our guide the desire to move from New York City to Jerusalem. She gets high marks for giving the most informative and interesting tour on the antiquities of the tunnel ever. She shows us a model of what Mt. Moriah looked like before Solomon built the Temple Mount. Then she explains how Herod expanded the Temple

---

21 A Mikvah is a purification bath taken by Jews before or after certain occasions.

Mount platform for his impressive temple. Next, we get a little history lesson. Romans destroyed the Second Temple in 70 AD, but left the Western Wall standing. Over the next 1,900 years, even during the most dangerous times, Jews risked their lives and property to make their way to the Wall. Throughout the millennia, the Wall remains a place where Jews come to pour their hearts out to God.

One of the most incredible parts of the tour features the size and beauty of the largest stone – the master course stone. The stone, 41 feet long, 15 feet deep, 11.5 feet tall, weighs over 500 metric tons. The master course stone shows the dedication of Herod and the Jews building the Temple. If they took so much care with a stone in the retaining wall to make it beautiful, we can only imagine the craftsmanship going into the Temple itself. The master course stone and all the walls remain as a Jewish style 'standing stone' to remind each generation of what transpired before. The top of the huge master course stone was destroyed in 70AD. Unlike the Temple and most of the walls, the Romans could not break this stone. Too massive for the Roman Army, it remains. The damage done to this stone in the retaining wall stands as a testimony to the Roman determination to wipe out the Jews and Temple worship. In spite of everything, Jews worship at this holy site today. God is faithful! This massive stone bears witness to His faithfulness.

You can pray at the closest point a Jew can get to the Holy of Holies. Orthodox Jews accept banishment from the Temple Mount. Rabbis forbid it because no one knows the exact location of the Holy of Holies. No Jew wants to risk entering the Holy of Holies by mistake. God's penalty for that, described in the Torah, is death. *"The Lord said to Moses: 'Tell your brother Aaron not to come whenever he chooses into the Most Holy Place behind the curtain in front of the atonement cover on the ark, or else he will die, because I appear in the cloud over the atonement cover'"* (Leviticus 16:2).

Our Jewish tour guide encourages each of us to stop at this holy place. This particular spot, underground in the Western Wall tunnel, gets us closer to the Holy of Holies than prayer places at the Wall outside. Ten years ago, our official tour guide seemed disinterested in prayer. We quickly passed by this sacred spot then. Today, we focus on this site. David spends meaningful time here. He dons his kippa and prays the Aaronic blessing over me in Hebrew.

"The Lord bless you and keep you, the Lord make his face shine upon you and be gracious unto you; the Lord turn his face toward you and give you peace." His heart soars and his tears well up. We spend time in personal prayer at this very special place before moving on.

David prays at spot closet to the Holy of Holics.

The tour ends as we step out onto the sunlit Via Dolorosa. This street is well known as the street Jesus walked while carrying the cross to his crucifixion. Stations of the Cross line it, commemorating events that happened during Jesus' walk. The Via Dolorosa occupies the Muslim

Quarter. For the first time since we arrived, I find myself in the Muslim Quarter. My comfort level drops to zero. The numerous stories studied, both fiction and non-fiction, portray this as a dangerous quarter of the Old City. My studies invariably lead to a greater understanding of the Jewish people. History, including comparably recent events, pits Muslims against Jews. I proudly confess my eternal support of Jews. They remain God's chosen people. He made an everlasting covenant with them. Everlasting means forever. I am committed to these people. Here I stand in the quarter of the Old City of the people who proclaim time after time Jews should not be in the land.

My mind considers the other side. For centuries, Jew and Muslim worked together side by side. Muslim leader, Suleiman the Magnificent, rebuilt the spectacular walls around Jerusalem in 1538. Suleiman made beneficial contributions to Jerusalem and the Israeli people. Not all Muslims hate Jews and Christians. Terrorist and extremists exist in all factions of society. I relax as I consider these positive images. I think of my sweet Muslim friends back home. They are family to us. They are just wonderful people who happen to be of the Muslim faith. We love them dearly and would be devastated if anything catastrophic happened to them. In fact, we pray for them constantly.

Countless shops make it more crowded here than the rest of the souk. Our tour group is instructed to wait for armed guards to escort us back to the Jewish Quarter. That in itself is somewhat frightening. We wait. David and I are beyond fatigue by now. It has been a long day of walking cobblestones, stairs, tunnels, steep streets, and just standing. We fall behind the group. Soldiers walk fast. No matter, the only danger has to do with pushy shopkeepers. We trudge past them.

We must hustle now. We have a date with the Wallcam and Craig. Later, Craig reports he saw David at the Wall and captured it. He promises to email the picture. Upon leaving the wall, David glances at the long staircase leading out of the plaza. He opts to take a taxi back to the Gloria. I could kiss him! He is my hero, again. Once back at the Gloria, we happily join tour groups for the dinner buffet. Soon we cuddle up to our heating pads, ice bags and heavenly beds!

THE FIFTH DAY

THE SILVER SCROLL

"The Lord bless you and keep you; the Lord make his face shine upon you and be gracious unto you; the Lord turn his face toward you and give you peace" (Numbers 6:24-26).

I wake up happy. I slept all night again! My sore body quickly reminds me of the pain I endured on the 1998 site studies. Then I lived on pain relievers. This trip we did not even bring a bottle. Getting out of bed forces my rebellious muscles to move. A hot baking soda bath helps. Those cobblestone streets and steps throughout the Old City take their toll. David, almost fully recovered, gets up early. He prays and then studies Hebrew before I even open my eyes. Smiling and enthusiastic, he begins planning for the day. I plan, too, for a quiet day of rest. He humors me. We languish over a cup of coffee upstairs until my third cup of coffee kicks in and signals it's time to leave.

The relaxing feels good, but soon my ADD kicks in. My mind turns to things we need to do. We should get some stamps at the post office, and then maybe have lunch. Yes, pizza sounds good. Soon we pause in the hotel lobby. I start taking pictures of the new entrance, new bar, meeting rooms, and new front courtyard. The management bustles about in readiness for the Pope's arrival tomorrow. We head for the post office. As soon as we get to the square at Jaffa Gate, vendors start in on us, "Come into my shop, let me show you..., won't you let me be your guide to the city?"

I'm used to their pushiness, and boldly reply, "No, we're going to the post office. We know where we're going."

One man tests, "Where is it then?"

I point ahead (as if I have to prove it), "We've been here before."

He shrugs and ambles off as we continue on our errands for the day. There's a noticeable upgrade in security. Armed soldiers and police appear everywhere we look. Earlier, when we left the Gloria, we read a sign posted on the door of a restaurant across the street, "We are closed in order to serve his Holiness..." I wonder what a chef decides to prepare for the Pope. Perhaps the Pope would enjoy my baked cabbage recipe. If he ever comes to my house, I'll fix it for him. Since he's in Jerusalem, he might consider having a falafel!

We turn down the cobblestone steps of David Street. Eisenberg says David Street is the "Hebrew name of the Old City known in Arabic as El-Bazaar."[22] Either that's the truth, or Eisenberg has a sense of humor! It's all shops and vendors everywhere you look. David Street commemorates King David, the beloved King of Israel. I also love the name David, because my wonderful husband is David, meaning beloved. David is my beloved, my *beshert*. By now, we have come to ignore the pushy vendors and gravitate to those infrequent vendors with a quieter demeanor. A man from Santa Monica, California runs one such shop. "I appreciate the fact that Americans like to window shop and that's all right with me," he says in greeting.

"How much is that menorah pendant in roman glass?"

"$100," he says at first, then changes his mind, "$80."

We ask about another piece of jewelry. His answer confirms our suspicion that we got ripped off a few days earlier. Not much, but enough to remind us to keep on our toes! Yesterday, a woman gave us a lesson in how to bargain. "You know how to bargain, don't you?" she asked. "You leave. Just leave and the price drops dramatically."

We get to test this today. We plan attending an outdoor event this week at night. Off we go to search for hooded sweat shirts. At the corner of David Street and Christian Quarter Road there's an interesting T-shirt shop run by a little old man with only one arm. He begins the same sales push the others do, so we start to step away. The woman was right. Boom! The price drops like the stock market in 2008! After the initial bargaining, the man shows his expertise. He helps us find transfers we like to iron on our shirts. I choose a long sleeved T-shirt and a message about loving everybody. "Love is like five loaves and two fish, always too little until you start giving it away." The shirt now depicts the miracle of Jesus when He multiplied five loaves and two fishes to feed a crowd of five thousand men plus women and children. You can read all about it in the Book of

---

22 Reprinted from *Streets of Jerusalem* with permission of Devora Publishing.

Matthew 14:17-21. I love reading about miracles Jesus performed. David picks a hooded sweatshirt and adds the Old City skyline to it. Our salesman allows David to take his picture with me.

We continue down Christian Quarter Road, stopping here and there, looking for a Bedouin bag. None are just right. Nearly at the end of Christian Quarter Road, David spies the place that helped him the day he went out by himself and got lost. Murad Ozgul, the young man who walked him back to the Gloria, introduces himself. He also introduces us to other family members working at the shop. They offer us drinks. I have orange juice instead of the strong Turkish coffee most of them drink. These shops, passed down generation by generation, often support several families. Brothers, cousins, uncles, parents, in-laws, etc., turn up all over the place with other little sub (not sandwich) shops. They all belong in this interwoven tapestry called Jerusalem. Few women work in the souk. I wonder what they do when their kids leave home. Children and schools abound in Jerusalem. Murad offers us seats — a big plus in our minds. Let the shopping begin.

This Messianic Jewelry shop sells many interesting items. David buys me a beautiful silver ring with the Song of Solomon 2:16 inscribed on it in Hebrew, *"my beloved is mine and I am his."* I am truly his, David's. He is the love of my life and God's gift to me. This shop makes a pendant like the scroll found near the Old City with the Aaronic Blessing written on it. That silver scroll contains the oldest Bible verse found so far.

In 1979, Gabriel Barkay, a Biblical archaeologist, chose to dig on the hill where St. Andrew's Church is located in the Hinnom Valley, just outside the Old City walls, where he discovered these silver scrolls. When Craig and I were students at Jerusalem University College, this relatively recent discovery in archaeological circles excited everyone. Barkay found an amulet with the tiny silver scroll inside. It took three years to unroll it without damaging it. Barkay dates the scroll to the seventh century BC, the time of King Josiah. This proves the books of the Pentateuch (Genesis, Exodus, Leviticus, Numbers and Deuteronomy) existed before then. This exciting find contains the Aaronic blessing found in Numbers 6:24-26, *"The Lord bless you and keep you; the Lord make his face shine upon you and be gracious unto you; the Lord turn his face toward you and give you peace."* This tiny scroll predates the earliest Dead Sea Scrolls by four hundred years!

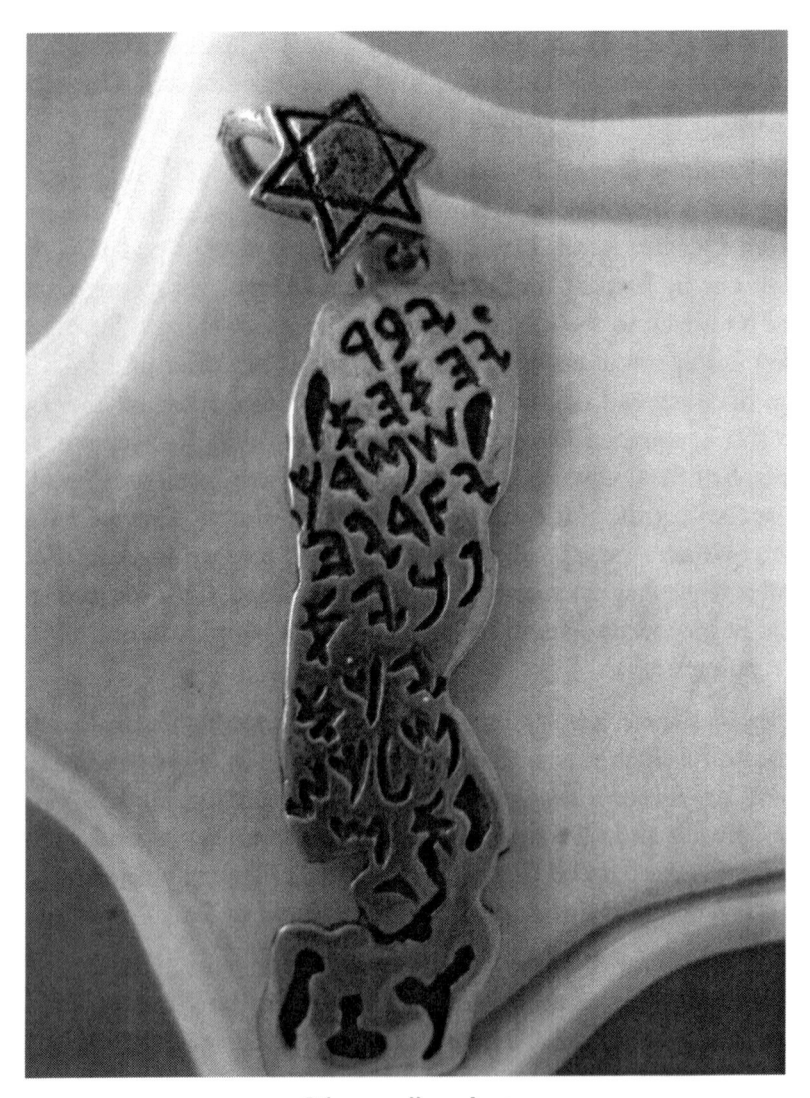

Silver scroll pendant.

The Aaronic Blessing, or the Priestly Blessing, provided by God blesses his people. He instructed the Hebrew Priests to use this blessing. Synagogues end their services with it. In our own Messianic Hebraic roots congregation, we always end the service with this extraordinary blessing. Jewish fathers bless their children at the end of a Shabbat meal using this blessing.

David introduces me to Issa Gadevky, our salesman. His name is Turkish and means Jesus. Issa speaks Aramaic. He recites the Lord's

Prayer in the ancient language Jesus spoke, reading it off a postcard, and ends up giving us two copies. Murad and Issa allow me to take a picture of them with David. I discover David emailed these fellows for several months before we arrived. He practically knew Murad before the first day he wandered into their shop – lost.

Two men in long priestly robes drop by. They speak another language. I try to make out any word I might know. No, it isn't Hebrew. Not English for sure, and it doesn't seem Arabic (by now we recognize some different languages). Issa kindly introduces us, "These are my priests; they are French." Out on the street, lots of people file by singing beautifully. "Those are the singers here from Poland to sing for the Pope."

Given what I hear, the Pope is in for a treat! Speaking of treat, I'm hungry and want to find a nice place to have pizza. Issa recommends a great place only a "five minute walk" from the shop. David and I eye each other suspiciously. A five minute walk for these guys could easily be half an hour for us. With sore feet, weak knees, and ADD, it seems risky. Issa senses our apprehension and quickly volunteers Murad to escort us. Always gracious, Murad claims he must visit someone at the hospital and is going that direction anyway.

Yerevon's Pizza sits in the Christian Quarter near New Gate. A cute little place, it boasts four tables. The menu offers grilled chicken pizza that includes grilled chicken, cheese, and black olives. Sounds good to me, but David doesn't like black olives so he asks the man if he could have the black olives just on one side. The pizza arrives. Obviously, something has been lost in translation. It has chicken, olives, and cheese on one side and the other side has cheese and *just* olives! So "olives on just one side" got translated to "nothing but olives on one side." No problem, David picks all the olives off the chicken side. Lunch is delicious!

There's a grill out front. The young man makes crepes spread with chocolate. We pass on those for today. The pizza place offers something in common with the Christian Jewelry store - no hurrying. We linger over two hours. Time goes quickly because the restaurant sits near New Gate and we're busy doing some serious people watching. We observe men in priestly or monk robes riding motorcycles. Tourists pour in behind their guides, looking this way and that, trying to take it all in at once. The locals stroll or hurry by nodding to each other. Press and photographers come by, here on assignment to follow the Pope. Secret service and police check stores for possible threats. And here we sit, in the midst of it all, in the City of Peace, enjoying pizza.

We start back to the Gloria via the Latin Patriarchate, the Pope's destination tomorrow. Barricades appear. David asks one of the men in front of the Latin Patriarchate why the barricades block our way.

"Don't you know the Pope is coming tomorrow?" The man looks at us as if we're crazy.

We squeeze by the barricades and make our way down the narrow street, made even narrower by more barricades. Because the barricades extend past the Gloria, we trudge all the way to Jaffa Square to go around them and back up to the entrance. Security allows no one on the streets, and I mean no one, from 11:00 a.m. to 4:00 p.m. tomorrow. The Israelis fear that a suicide bomber might try to harm the Pope. David hopes we get a peek at the Pope. I find it incredible that God gives a mere man a position of such power and spiritual responsibility. Make no mistake about that – only God gives kings, presidents, or Popes power.

Once back to our familiar little nest, we rest. As sore as I was this morning, I can hardly believe how far we went today. For dinner we fix instant shakes in the room and write in our journals. In a few minutes we will play cards. I have every intention of beating David! Yes, the love of my life!

The Sixth Day

Lag B'Omer

"From the day after the Sabbath, the day you brought the sheaf of the wave offering, count off seven full weeks" (Leviticus 23:15).

"You are my perfect gift from God," the card says. Truer sentiment could not be expressed. I picked it out before we came and carefully hid it for today. It's David's birthday. The Pope arrives later. Yesterday, David joked for his birthday he would like the Pope to come by and sing Happy Birthday to him. He gets part of his wish. The Pope comes by our hotel. The Papal visit is no small undertaking. I wonder how many millions it cost the State of Israel in security alone. The security we witness from our hotel is amazing. This morning we get to the dining room a few minutes early. Food is still on the buffet, but the dining room has no patrons sitting at tables. The dining room manager tells us the Pope is coming. Everyone left while they could still get out. Okay. I guess that doesn't sink in until later.

We eat breakfast and enjoy the pleasant quiet. Suddenly from outside, two stories below, we hear Latin singing. Our wait staff runs to the windows yelling, "Viva, viva!" The same words echo back to them. "Viva, viva!" Over fifty men dressed in black robes traverse the narrow street toward the Latin Patriarchate. They chant a joyful song. People join in. Like something out of an Italian musical, joy fills the air. Faces light up. Eyes sparkle. The Pope is coming!

Back in our nest, we check out Wallcam to see what happens for Lag B'Omer.[23] Lag B'Omer is celebrated in several different ways depending on the age, situation, and devoutness of the person. Some people celebrate by building huge bonfires. The younger folks enjoy this activity. Youngsters gather anything wood to burn. This means contractors throughout Israel must hire additional guards to protect wooden building supplies. Wooden planks and scaffolding make breathtaking bonfires! Fortunately, the traditional wood gathering begins only about 10 days before the holiday.

---

23 Lag B'Omer's literal translation means the 33rd day of the Omer. Omer is a measure of barley. The festival is found in the Torah (Leviticus 23:15-16).

Lag B'Omer is somewhat of a lesser holiday. It occurs between Passover, which celebrates the deliverance of the Jews from Egypt via crossing the Red Sea as on dry land, and Shavuot, which commemorates Moses coming down Mt. Sinai with the Ten Commandments. The counting reminds us of the connection between Passover and Shavuot. According to the Torah, *"From the day after the Sabbath, the day you brought the sheaf of the wave offering, count off seven full weeks"* (Leviticus 23:15). This period celebrates the counting of the Omer. On the second day of Passover, an Omer of barley is cut and brought to the Temple as a wave offering.

Every night from the second night of Passover to the night before Shavuot[24], Jews recite a blessing and state the count of the Omer in both weeks and days. For instance, on the 15th day you would say, "Today is 15 days, which is two weeks and one day of the Omer." The counting reminds Jews that redemption didn't just happen at the Red Sea. Completion hinged on their receiving the Ten Commandments.

In the second century, Rabbi Akiva developed the exegetical method that links each traditional Jewish practice back to a basis in a Biblical text. He is justly called the father of the Mishnah.[25] Rabbi Akiva taught "love your neighbor as yourself – this is the great principle of the entire Torah." Sadly, in about 132 AD during the counting of the Omer, twenty four thousand of Rabbi Akiva's students died in a divinely sent plague. Jews believe God sent the plague because the students did not show honor to one another. The plague ended on the 33rd day of counting the Omer. The Hebrew letters Lamed and Gimmel create the acronym "lag," which has the numerical value of 33. Lag B'Omer became the holiday celebrating God's grace in stopping the plague. Rabbi Akiva began teaching again with a few students who survived the plague and continued to have a great effect on Jewish Torah thinking.

Rabbi Akiva's students disagreed with each other about small details of Torah application. Jesus commanded His disciples to love one another (John 13:34). Do our disagreements between Protestant denominations show honor to one another? We learn from Lag B'Omer that loving all denominations and the Jews is critical.

24 Shavuot or Shavuos commemorates the day Moses brought the Ten Commandments down from Mt. Sinai. It is also referred to as the Festival of Weeks, Day of the First Fruits, or Festival of Reaping.
25 The Mishnah teaches the oral traditions by example, primarily using examples brought to judgment by rabbis.

Meanwhile, back at Wallcam, the vacated men's prayer section shows three priests in white robes. Many people outside the area watch. So many people logged onto the live Wallcam feed that no more can watch. Even during the Independence Day Celebration speeches at the Kotel with the flame and honor guards, we could log on to the live feed. Something big must be happening, but we have no idea what. We will check out the Jewish Quarter when we can leave.

We load up our portable chairs, snacks, jackets, and IDs to take to the streets. I glance across the courtyard and see armed Israeli soldiers jogging up the stairs of the opposite wing of our hotel. Other officers, Israeli police on the roof and city ramparts, prepare for the Pope's arrival. Things get serious now. We venture past the front desk to the front courtyard where two IDF (Israeli Defense Force) soldiers armed with machine guns block our exit.

"You cannot pass." No smiles, either. David asks if we could just go out and sit behind the barricades. They laugh and shake their heads. They get their jollies at our expense. David asks if he will be able to take a picture of the Pope. This time they laugh hysterically, speak a few unrecognizable words, and clutch their sides, laughing again.

Soldiers block our exit from the Gloria.

Then, dead serious again, one soldier repeats, "No, you cannot leave." No one can enter or leave. At 10:00 a.m., we seem trapped. The Pope, nowhere near our street, won't get here until 12:30 p.m. or so. He must be at the Wall. Later, we find out the entire Old City shut down. Shops remain closed. Streets deserted. Our street teems with all sorts of security personnel. Since we cannot leave, we find a window near the pre-renovation entrance halfway up a staircase that affords us an enticing view. As far as I can tell, three or four types of security walk up and down our tiny street. First, the IDF with automatic weapons wearing army green uniforms, look scariest. Then, officers in blue, the Israeli police, carry handguns and sometimes machine guns. Men, wearing black suits and sunglasses with coiled wires hanging out of their ears could be MIB (Men In Black) or maybe secret service, watch windows and roof tops. Finally, the friendliest kind of security sniffs at our window and discovers David with his camera. The bomb sniffing dog alerts his handler. The soldier peers in at David.

"Is it O.K.?" David asks.

The officer says, "Yes."

Relieved he at least passed the bomb squad; David gets aggressive about taking pictures. He gets some great video footage.

With over two hours to wait, I go back to the hotel dining room to get pictures of my own. The security on the ramparts directly across looks impressive. I take the shot, spin around to leave, and look directly into the eyes of an IDF soldier toting an Uzi! I throw my open hands into the air and smile. The camera dangles from my wrist. Seeing a harmless tourist, the two soldiers move on. Unnerved, I find my way back to David. These soldiers are heavily armed, big, and move about silently. I would not want to be in a war type situation with any one of them, unless of course they were on my side!

David tells me about the sniffing bomb dog incident. I relate what happened to me in the dining room. We huddle by the window. The wrought iron decoration on the open window frustrates me. I keep whispering, "I missed that shot," or "I got a good shot at this or that." Then I remind myself, *it is not a good time to refer to taking pictures as shooting!* We get some great shots of security forces and even a few priestly personnel on their way to lunch with the Pope. Every one of the two hundred fifty attendees must pass by this window to get to the Pope's luncheon.

Our gracious hotel manager mentions he can open a room directly upstairs if I would like a better view. David loves his little perch on the stairs. The little nook looks quite comfortable with his tri-pod, jacket, water, and snacks. He thinks the wrought iron decoration that so frustrates me adds uniqueness to his photographs. I find the upstairs window better. I set up a chair and position my camera for some great shots – oops! (*I've got to stop using that word.*) Around 12:30 p.m., the men in black suits begin talking into their shoulders. Right on time, the Pope in a black windowed limo passes our window. The barricade at the bottom of our street disappears. One by one, five cars pass by, guards on either side of each one. We can only speculate about the one in which the Pope rides. David gets great video of the whole 60 second phenomenon. We find ourselves within ten feet of the Pope. Now, we wait until he finishes lunch and leaves. Then we can leave the hotel.

Personnel, made up of security, press, or people late for mass, immediately run up the hill. The barricades close again until around 3:30 p.m. We keep busy. Back in our courtyard we review pictures and videos, and write in our journals. We enjoy the fountain, birds, and blooming flowers. Time passes quickly. Once we know we can leave, it seems obligatory. We head down our little street away from the souk at David Street and up the small side street into the Armenian Quarter.

The Armenian Quarter is the smallest quarter in the Old City. It reminds me of the Armenian Holocaust that included killing, torture, starvation, and death marches from around 1896-1923. Few people acknowledge the Armenian Holocaust, but Armenians report losses of 1,500,000 people at the hands of the Turks. Over 1,600 churches were destroyed. The first Armenians lived in Jerusalem in 95AD. They share the violent history of the city.

We met an Armenian Christian who lived in the Armenian Quarter his entire life. His family moved here in 1917 when they escaped the Armenian Holocaust. They lived in the same house during the British Mandate, before and after the 1948 Israeli War of Independence, before and after the 1967 War, and still live there today. Unlike Jews, as Christians they have been able to live in the Old City continuously since 1917. He has an interesting perspective on politics since his family has lived through so many wars and regime changes. He loves Israel and likes Netanyahu, but is wary of Obama. He thinks Jerusalem should be an international city, like Switzerland. How to do that safely is a mystery.

Today, the Armenian Quarter makes for a quiet change from aggressive shopkeepers and sales vendors on David Street and in the Muslim Quarter. No one here races out to drag you into their 'new' shop. Only a few shops stay open due to the Pope's visit. We duck in to see if any of them have anything unique to offer. We want lunch more than anything and find our way back to Cardo Pizza. Yes, we have pizza again, but at another shop. This shop, Cardo Pizza, and another shop all share a small plaza near the Cardo. You can choose from twelve tables. Each shop has four tables. Cardo Pizza uses aluminum tables, the shop we buy from uses wood tables, and the shop across the way uses yellow tables. The system works because a grouchy old man will shoo you away if you sit in the wrong place!

The young man who made our pizza comes out to visit with us. He asks if we are from the U.S. and what state. Born Israeli, he has lived out of the country and is anxious to leave again. He complains that Jerusalem is all about money. He says Jesus would throw everyone out, like He tossed the money changers out of the Temple.

"The Pope closed the city down so the shopkeepers lost money and yet none of them got to see his Holiness." He continues to kvetch until the grouchy old man sends him back to his store to wait on some new customers. The customers happen to be two women Israeli soldiers.

After lunch, we stop by to see the Torah Scribe about our mezuzah scroll. He did not come in today. We stop at the nearby public restrooms. The restrooms have changed for the better in the last ten years. You can actually find rest rooms, but you had better bring your own TP. So far, I haven't found one with any in it!

Around the corner we visit the Moriah bookstore. This time I look for a prayer shawl for a woman back home. We need help because we aren't sure what size to get. Because prayer shawls are for men in the Jewish tradition, I don't feel like telling the salesman it is for a woman. So (forgive me, Lord) I concoct a story about buying a prayer shawl for my nephew's bar-mitzvah! "How tall is he?" asks our helper.

"He's about your height," I tell him.

"Oh, he's a big boy!"

"Yes, for his age he is tall." My face turns red. With the nice man's help, we find the perfect tallit for my *nephew*. A traditional shawl with the Israeli blue stripes, I know she'll love it.

I want to get David tallit clips for his birthday. The ones David and Murad designed earlier remain in process. I find some he likes with the Old City pictured and Jerusalem written in Hebrew. We leave the Moriah Bookstore walking toward the Western Wall. It's easy to get turned around in the Old City. Somehow, we end up in the Muslim Quarter. It's not scary like the other day. These guys are the most aggressive of all vendors. I race past, ignoring their invitations.

One man yells "Come into my shop and give me a chance to rip you off." This unique technique does not impress me. We see a nice, not pushy, young man. I step into his shop and tell him I am looking for a thimble. A friend of mine from Denver requested I bring back a thimble from Jerusalem for her collection. So far, I have not found one, but this man has several. For only 15 NIS I get her one with a cityscape of Jerusalem around it. I spot imitation roman glass another friend wanted. None of it is in the shape of a tear bottle. I decide to press on. However, the lad refuses to take no for an answer. He goes from little bottles to jewelry. He shows us a Star of David on a silver chain. This amazing piece has what looks like crushed opal in the star. When you tug on the chain, the star comes apart and makes an entirely different necklace. It is truly unique. About then, his father comes into the shop and gets busy with something else. The son continues to work with us. He makes us such a deal. You know, because only few customers come in today with the Pope's visit and all.

He practically gives us this fine piece of jewelry for only 1,200 NIS ($300)!

I stand up, saying to David, "that's way too much, way out of our budget."

We start walking toward the entrance and he yells, "No, no, I *give* it to you – 800 shekels ($200)." Then his father gets in the picture and things begin to get ugly. To tell the truth, I never wanted it from the get go. It is pretty and unique, but quite truthfully I have way too much pretty and unique jewelry already.

The father says to me, in a syrupy voice, "Tell me the truth. How much will you spend? How much you pay?"

I say, "You're talking to the wrong person (sorry David) and the man immediately starts talking to David in loud voice.

I have to raise my voice to be heard, "David, I don't want it."

The man growls, yelling, "I'm talking to him – Sir, 300 shekels ($75)." I stomp out of the shop. David follows me. The man follows David. We start moving faster. We are practically running.

Three stores down the man is still behind us yelling, "I give it to you 200 shekels ($50), take it, I give it to you!" We run around the corner, down the street to the Wall plaza. But WOW!!! A 1,000 shekel ($250) drop in price! David estimates the poorly made necklace's true value at $20 - $25. We learn how to bargain at this shop! No matter how good the deal sounds, they still make money.

We arrive at the Wall and split up as David goes to the men's side to pray. On the women's side, I press my fingertips against the stone. The enormity of what God has done with the Jewish people and the nation of Israel overcomes me. I pray for their salvation, the peace of Jerusalem, and for His will to be done. I confess my sins and thank Him for a salvation of which I am not worthy. I thank Him for the awesome, gracious gift to us of this incredible adventure.

We meet back by the Israeli flag pole in the middle of the plaza and go out the security entrance toward the taxis. Since it is a holiday, we wait quite awhile for our turn. Finally, a taxi stops. I see the passenger side window go down and David speaks a few words and starts to get in beside the driver. I'm sitting twenty feet away on a short stone pillar. When I see David get in, I jump up and yank the back door open and – to my surprise – a Hassidic Jew is already firmly entrenched!

I jump back, "Sorry, I didn't see you." And of course I hadn't seen the man through the darkened window. Without a word, the young man scrambles to the other side of the cab. I am so glad to get a ride I actually keep my mouth shut the whole way and never so much as glance his way. Out of the corner of my eye I see his head bowed and his prayer book opened. The taxi drops us off down the hill from Jaffa Gate, and then tries to overcharge us. It is a short walk. Tired, our dogs barking, we make the difficult climb back to our nest in the Gloria.

We celebrate surviving greedy shopkeepers and taxi drivers with chocolate shakes and peanut butter in our room. We retire. I sleep better and longer than any other night. I'm pretty much back to my normal routine. David seems to be, too. Unbelievably, I forgot my walking shoes. My walking shoes wait in Colorado, sitting on a chair next to where I packed. I brought some old favorites to slog through Hezekiah's tunnel because of the rough surface beneath the flowing waters. Walking is harder than it should be. Tomorrow I use the cane.

THE SEVENTH DAY

THE HEBREW CONNECTION

"I ask then: Did God reject his people? By no means! I am an Israelite myself, a descendant of Abraham, from the Tribe of Benjamin" (Romans 11:1).

Today calls for rest and recuperation. Naturally I wake up early. The hot soak bath reminds my body life is good. I begin looking forward to our day. The empty dining room seems spacious. All the students and tour groups got an early start again. Good for them. The fresh fruit basket contains a few broken stems. It's nine o'clock and the kitchen crew wants to shut down. Rolls, scrambled eggs, cereal, something I can't describe (looks ugly, tastes very good), and coffee fuel me for the morning.

We write post cards, journal, check emails – including a Happy Birthday e-card for David. The card games we played yesterday didn't go as I expected. We each won one. I expect to fix that some time today.

David's great idea for lunch involves the restaurant across the street. They cooked for the Pope. Unfortunately, we find the place closed. Up the hill just a little way we reach another restaurant David researched. On the top ten restaurant list by Gila, Nafoura's comes highly recommended by Murad. Today's perfect weather warrants sitting on their patio. The restaurant serves yet another buffet. The roasted chicken and little yellow potatoes appeal to our American appetite. We share a table with two ladies we don't know. They don't speak one word to us. The ladies drink their tea quickly and head for the rest room. Soon after, a guide leaves taking his group with him, leaving us alone on the spacious outdoor patio. Everyone visiting Israel takes a tour to optimize their time here.

David calls the guide Weymuth, after our friend who puts tours together. David imagines him telling his group how lucky they are to eat at this fabulous restaurant on the patio next to the Old City wall. Nafoura's serves delicious food in a perfect Old City setting. The ancient Jerusalem stone wall around the city with ramparts on top serves as the back wall of the inviting courtyard. An awning and treetops hide the ramparts. Big yellow roses in the courtyard shade the mandatory cat.

Nafoura's garden patio.

Today I reflect on the reason I love Israel and the Jewish people so very much. My strong Christian faith anchors me. However, being grafted into Jewish roots gives me an undeniable connection to this Land, which God gave to the Hebrews so long ago. Christians and Jews have much in common. Christians agree with Jews that Adam was created, not evolved. We both believe in the One true God, the Lord God Almighty, Creator of the universe and everything in it. We agree, after God accomplished all these things, He rested on the seventh day.

The perfect world God created soon disintegrated. The world developed into something opposite of what God originally designed. It happened over a short period of time, alerting us to the speed of degeneration. I find it disconcerting when I think of the evil man efficiently renders. Jews refer to the evil inclination as Yetzer Hara, the inclination to do evil by violating God's will. God saw how wicked man had become. He decided

52

to destroy mankind because every one of them thought only of doing evil all the time. He regretted creating man. Instead of destroying everything and starting over, God found one righteous man on the face of the earth. God told Noah to build an ark. The Biblical account reports, *"Noah was six hundred years old when the flood waters came on the earth"* (Genesis 7:6). I'm not sure how long it took to build the ark, but that fact encourages me. When I start feeling too old to serve the Lord or anything else, I remember Noah. For a hundred and fifty days the earth remained flooded. Noah's family survived and repopulated the world. This true story told by Jewish and Christian believers underscores the graciousness of God.

The Christian faith acknowledges Abraham, Isaac, and Jacob as patriarchs of the faith. Jews and Christians share the same heroes of the faith. The twelve tribes[26], descendants of Jacob, make up the beginning of the descendants of Abraham. God promised these descendants that they would multiply and become, *"as numerous as the stars in the sky and as countless as the sand on the seashore."* We read about Sarah, Rachel, Leah, and Rebekah, the wives of the patriarchs, and marvel at their bravery and endurance. The account of Joseph's life is particularly inspiring. Joseph had every reason to be vengeful and bitter. He set those attitudes aside to serve the Lord. Moses, Aaron, Miriam, Jethro, Joshua, Caleb and other names become as familiar to Christian Sunday School children as they do to children who attend synagogue. All these accounts flow from the Torah.

We have Old Testament and Biblical history in common with the Jews. We read accounts of battles won and rejoice. We despair at times when God's people failed Him. We humbly accept His faithfulness to heal us and bring us to Him on His own terms.

Christians owe a great debt to present day Jews for preserving the traditions and feasts of the Lord. Jesus is a Jew. Long ago, He left us to go sit at the right hand of the Father. In order to better understand what He taught in the New Testament, we observe Jews today as they celebrate the same festivals and feasts Jesus did.

Interestingly enough, all the disciples, including the apostle Paul, claim Jewish heritage. Paul, a Pharisee before his conversion on the road to Damascus, enjoyed membership in the Sanhedrin. My own vision agrees

---

26 The twelve tribes of Israel are Reuben, Simeon, Levi, Judah, Dan, Naphtali, Gad, Asher, Issachar, Zebulun, Joseph, and Benjamin.

with that of Paul's. He believed the Church would encompass Jew and Gentile alike in their love for God. He believed Jew and Gentile would become one. Whatever one's heritage had been in the past would be immaterial. Belief in Christ would be all that mattered. We must remember not all Jews rejected Christ. Many more will accept Him in the future.

"God did not reject his people, whom he foreknew. Don't you know what the scripture says in the passage about Elijah – how he appealed to God against Israel: 'Lord, they have killed your prophets and torn down your altars; I am the only one left, and they are trying to kill me'" (Romans 11:2-3). God responded to Elijah by telling him seven thousand had not yet bowed to Baal. These represented God's remnant at that time. Today, a remnant of Jewish believers accepts Yeshua HaMashiachc, Jesus the Messiah! This remnant, chosen by the grace of God, brings blessing to the Jewish people and light to a dark world. By rejecting Christ when He first came, Jews didn't fall beyond recovery. Instead, they made salvation available to the Gentiles. Christians owe a great deal to the Jews.

Salvation stands foremost in the minds of Christians. The Scripture in Romans 11:26-29 lifts me, *"And so all Israel will be saved, as it is written: 'The deliverer will come from Zion; he will turn godlessness away from Jacob. And this is my covenant with them when I take away their sins. As far as the gospel is concerned, they are enemies on your account; but as far as election is concerned, they are loved on account of the patriarchs, for God's gifts and his call are irrevocable."* These verses say Jews remain loved on account of the patriarchs. God's gifts and His irrevocable call endure! Thirty-five hundred years ago, God gifted this land to the Hebrews (Jews). I confess I have always been desirous of the Jewish heritage, so rich and beyond imagination. The Old Testament reads like family history. Grafted in, I can say it's about my ancestors and their relationship to the Lord God Almighty. I admit as a young teen I told my friends Jewish blood ran through my veins. My way of identifying with Christ would change over time. In my teenage mind, I reasoned that if He is my brother, as in joint heirs with Christ, then I had to be Jewish. My maiden name, Myers, sounded Jewish, so I decided I was Jewish. No one in my family ever said we were Jewish. Back then I didn't know how to check it out. The other day a friend gave me a website with Jewish names on it (http://www.avotaynu.com/books/MenkNames.htm). I found my maiden name and my father's mother's name, Hill. So just maybe, hopefully, there's Jewish blood in me. For sure it runs through my heart. You might want to check it out for yourself.

We take time eating and then saunter back to the Gloria. Later we venture down to the bar to play cards for awhile. Yes! I beat David two out of two games. Finally, justice for the beatings I took earlier in the week!

The great thing about the time we spend at the bar, besides me winning, is that we actually get Pepsi Max[27] with ice. Getting ice for drinks doesn't happen often. We return to our room, find no emails, read and retire. It has been a quiet day, and "coincidentally" the seventh day of our trip. Even though we had not planned to rest on the seventh day of our trip, it happened naturally. *"Indeed, when Gentiles, who do not have the law, do by nature things required by the law, they are a law for themselves, even though they do not have the law, since they show that the requirements of the law are written on their hearts, their consciences also bearing witness, and their thoughts now accusing, now even defending them"* (Romans 2:14-15).

---

27 Pepsi Max is Jerusalem's version of Diet Pepsi. I like Diet Pepsi better than Diet Coke, so in Israel I chose Pepsi Max over Coke Zero. Pepsi Max is also available in many other countries and perhaps parts of the US.

THE EIGHTH DAY

THE CITADEL

*"This is what the Sovereign Lord says: On the day I chose Israel,
I swore with uplifted hand to the descendants of the house of Jacob
and revealed myself to them in Egypt. With uplifted hand I said to
them, 'I am the Lord your God.' On that day I swore to them that
I would bring them out of Egypt into a land I had searched out for
them, a land flowing with milk and honey, the most beautiful of all
lands" (Ezekiel 20:5-6).*

On May 14, 1948, Israel claimed its independence from Great Britain.
The very next day, five Arab nations attacked Israel. Those nations believed
Israel had no right to exist. Modern Israel's independence came at a heavy
price. That war divided Jerusalem, the city of peace, into East and West
Jerusalem. Jordan held East Jerusalem. Today is the 14th of May. I expect
some kind of celebration. Checking the Jerusalem Post online, I find no
mention of the historic event. David says Israel uses the Jewish (lunar)
calendar to determine some holidays. Thus, the celebration of Israel's
independence happened earlier in the month.

Today we explore the Citadel. People look at the minaret today and
call it the Tower of David. Our guidebook dates the confusion to the
Byzantine era when they mistakenly identified this area as the City of
David. However, the tower wasn't constructed until 1655. Sometimes the
facts suck the romantic notions you have right out of you! The Tomb of
David sits a stone's throw away. It's still the Tower of David to me.

An American tour group fills the dinning room this morning. Instead
of leaving, we people watch. Finally we stroll back to our nest and gather
the gear we need for a day out. This means snacks, hats, jackets (just in
case), water, tissues, cameras, note pads, pens, and so forth. My wonderful
heating pad quit. We stop by the nearby pharmacy to get a new one.
Nothing is simple here. Of course, they don't have one. They will order
one. It will come later in the day. The woman waiting on us mentions the
Pope returns in the morning and they will be closed all day. This time

the Pope comes up the street on the other side of us to the Church of the Holy Sepulcher. "Every time they come and shut the Old City down. Condoleeza Rice, she came so many times. What did she do? Nothing. There will never be peace," the woman complains.

In unison, David and I encourage her, "Until the Lord comes," and she agrees, "Yes, when the Lord comes." We have a good conversation. It lifts my spirits. My heart sings as I remember the Lord is coming back for us and, when He does, there will be lasting peace here.

We peek in the store across the street. Although we've walked past here several times, I had not noticed this particular store. He sells beads and stones for necklaces. David seems interested, but we need to move on. We need to buy a birthday card for our daughter in-law, Gina. The small pharmacy does not have cards, so we try the Christian Book Store just across the entrance from the Citadel. A nice man here helps us find a card for Gina. He even writes "Happy Birthday" in Hebrew inside. I add a short note. We are off to the post office next door. I find doing errands without a car refreshing. We buy and mail the card quicker here than we would back home with a car.

We cross the busy street, go up the ramp, and enter the Citadel. We choose from three tours: Archaeology, Exhibits, and Panoramic. Panoramic means lots of steps up. Archaeology means lots of steps down. We choose Exhibits situated on the middle level. After buying our tickets, they direct us to take a right and watch an introductory film. I like films. For the most part they inform, take place in warm or cool rooms, and best of all contain comfy chairs! We cheerfully take the first right and behold two flights of ancient stairs. Oh, well! This factual yet concise animated production about Jerusalem impresses us. We step out of the little theater and up a few more ancient steps onto the 2,000-year old tower, giving us a beautiful view of the city and the ancient courtyard.

Citadel's ancient courtyard from Phasael Tower.

This amazing courtyard contains archaeological remains from almost every era from the second century BC to the twelfth century AD. Excavations indicate a fortress from the time of Herod. This is the most likely site of Christ's trial and condemnation. We look down from the top of Phasael Tower, built by Herod the Great, named after his brother. Hadrian destroyed it in 135AD. It was partially rebuilt in the 14th century. A group of about 20 Muslim girls in school uniforms crowd around their teacher in front of us. They study the model of the Citadel built on a 1/100 scale. General Allenby accepted the surrender of the Turks in 1917 here at the Citadel.

The peaceful Citadel today makes it hard to imagine before the 1967 Six-Day War, soldiers stood on these walls. They took sniper shots at Jews standing on Mt. Zion yearning to glimpse the Old City walls and pray to Hashem (God). Today it operates as a museum and cultural center instead of a fort. It stands as a testimony, not only of the history of the site, but of the vision of Teddy Kollek, former mayor of Jerusalem who took on the responsibility for many restorations in the Old City.

We tour through the Canaanite Period, the First Temple Period, Return to Zion, and Second Temple Period (including an absolutely fantastic model of Herod's Temple), through late Roman and Byzantine Periods, the (more boring) Islamic Period, the (sad) Crusader Period, Ayyubid Period, Mamluk, and Ottoman Periods. Finally we get to the British Mandate. We've covered a whole lot of history. In between, I get side tracked and *accidentally* do the Panoramic Tour. I confess the views of Jerusalem enticed me to climb the extra stairs. We take a break.

David buys me a cold soda with a chocolate brownie. We sit and relax in the middle of the historical fortress. I excuse myself to go to the rest room, take a wrong turn coming back and *accidentally* take the Archaeological tour. I love archaeology. At last, the end room is a synopsis of the last one hundred years of the city. Jewish immigrants and Christians came to settle outside the city walls inaugurating the modern city of Jerusalem.

Thankfully, I have my hat. The hot sun reflects off the white stone walls and arches. During rest times we meet two ladies. The exhausted first one reminds me of when David and I came on tour ten years ago. This woman travels with Kay Arthur's Precepts Tour. She hails from Wichita, Kansas. Another lady on the same tour, a retired schoolteacher, tired and a bit cranky, hails from North Carolina. I ask her if they have a free day. "This is it," she groans. Ah, yes, I remember it well, and *thank God* David and I decided to do it our way – slowly! Believe me, plenty of guides volunteer help every day. With David's thorough research and attitude of preparedness, along with maps and books, we don't need them! (Not to mention the Lord's good graces upon us.) We close the place down at 4:00p.m., having spent the entire day here, doing all of the offered tours.

Walking back to the Gloria, I can't help but recount the history of Jerusalem. How many times has this city risen from defeat? How soon will we see the new, glorified Jerusalem, lit by His very presence?

Dinner at the Gloria always satisfies. Every table taken, the American tourists and students enjoy the delights of the dining room. People-watching makes waiting fun. After dinner we take a stroll down David Street to the souk. The shops begin closing. IDF soldiers and their bomb sniffing dogs prepare for the arrival of the Pope. Only a few vendors try forcing us into their shops. One fellow humors us. We go in just to look.

Because we start leaving without purchasing anything, he raises his voice. "OK you go now. I'm closing, you go now." As we walk down the street he yells, "If you change your mind, I be open only one hour!" Yes, the Old City. We begin to enjoy its rhythm.

We go down Christian Quarter Road. It becomes obvious we will either walk down narrow residential streets in the dark or we should turn back and retrace our steps out of the Old City souk. Guard dogs and soldiers convince us to turn back. Once out of the souk, we venture out of Jaffa Gate into the modern city. We cross over the four-lane highway into a very different type of shopping mall. It looks like the 16th Street shopping mall in downtown Denver. We roam the wide pedestrian streets, sit on some steps, and watch people in the bars and coffee shops. I check out some dress shops looking for a dress to wear in my sister Cynthia's wedding. She postponed her wedding until we return. As soon as we get back to Colorado, we must drive to Topeka to participate joyfully in her wedding. We look forward to it, but I must shop in Jerusalem for the dress because of time constraints. Nothing seems appropriate. Everything seems expensive. I refuse to spend more on my dress than the bride spends on hers.

We walk upstairs to a broad plaza. We can see the light show at the citadel, which we plan on attending some other night. Two boys kick a soccer ball back and forth. The older boy trains the younger one. Both play well and never touch the ball with their hands. My gaze drifts off to the lights of modern Jerusalem. All of a sudden, the ball hits my leg "Slicha (excuse me)," the boy says.

"Beseder (its ok)," David replies. It stings, but there is no real injury. We wander back to the hotel. It's some distance and I remember that earlier, after dinner while I rested, David went back to the pharmacy to get my new heating pad. The one they got in at the nearby pharmacy wasn't right, so David (with his bad knee) sneaked down here to the Super Pharmacy (which is the size of Walgreen's back home) and found one. The Super Pharmacy stands in the middle of this huge new modern mall below the impromptu soccer field. David really does take good care of me. Thank You, Yeshua!! He's my blessing from You.

THE NINTH DAY

THE GARDEN TOMB

"He himself bore our sins in his body on the tree, so that we might die to sins and live for righteousness; by his wounds you have been healed" (I Peter 2:24).

Breakfast buffet offers the same good food as always. We have our own routine, too. During breakfast we decide what we want to do that day. With no set itinerary, we enjoy each day however we choose. The freedom rejuvenates David, who lives a scheduled life. Today we get our favorite table by the windows. Only three other people sit. Four more arrive while we dine. The tour groups got out early again because of the Pope's second visit to the Old City this week. I settle in and enjoy the solitude, the fantastic view of the King David Hotel over the ramparts, tasty bread and honey, eggs, and three cups of coffee.

We decide to walk up to Mt. Zion where Craig and I took our class at Jerusalem University College. We pack up our gear and head out. Barricades block our path. We try to convince soldiers if they let us pass, we will turn away from the Old City and the Church of the Holy Sepulcher (the Pope's destination). Since we are the last street on the perimeter, we think they just might do it. But no, we must wait, and *no pictures*! These soldiers look serious. Looking past them, I see why. Army and Security personnel jam Jaffa Gate and the street leading into the Old City. We trudge back up the hill to the Gloria. An old man stops us and helpfully says, "You can get out by New Gate." Thanks for the choice, but we have no intention of walking that far. We opt for returning to our quiet courtyard to read and write. Time slips away.

We snack for lunch. Maybe it is safe to go out now. Success! No barricades, the streets teem with tourists and vendors. We risk death by pedestrian-car accident crossing the street to get a taxi. We want to go to the Garden Tomb. David says the taxi should cost us about 30 shekels. When the taxi driver says 50 shekels, I say "No!" and start walking away.

The driver immediately says he will do it by meter. David refuses, thinking the guy will take the long way.

The driver says, "Look, the traffic is bad. I do it for 40 shekels." Indeed, the traffic is horrible. We readily agree.

On the way, David chats with the driver. The man lives in the West Bank. He tries to convince us to let him take us outside the city, like a little private tour. David tells him we planned this trip for a year and have done much research. We know what we want to do and where we want to go. He can just let us off at the street below the Garden Tomb. He does. As we plod up the steep, narrow road, I comment to myself on how quiet it seems. Soon we arrive at the closed doors of the Garden Tomb. Closed! I laugh and aloud saying, "We planned this trip for a year, we studied. We know everything." mocking David's conversation with our taxi driver. I just know the driver knew! David laughs, "Details are important," he mocks himself with one of his favorite slogans.

The Garden Tomb opens at 2:00 p.m. We have a couple of hours to spend exploring this area of town. We stand a couple of blocks from the Muslim Quarter's Damascus Gate. I survey those towers where the Jordanian snipers stood prior to the Six-Day War, randomly shooting at Jews who might be unfortunate enough to be within range. We start toward the towers when I have a *moment*.

"David, I remember this street. The shopkeepers, the merchandise, fresh fruits and vegetables out on the street bring it all back. Mostly I remember the bakery and all types of loaves of breads sitting on carts on the sidewalk." In 1999, Mom was with us. We observed all this activity. I remember being glad we were on the bus. After all, this is the Arab area. Since then, my fears have greatly diminished.

Actually, some of the shopkeepers here act nicer than in the Old City souk. They don't drag you into their shops and yell at you. However, I notice some people tend to ignore you on purpose. Several young men bump into me with their shoulder, rather forcefully. Regaining my balance, I keep going without so much of an "excuse me" in Arabic or any language. Because of the crowds, I prefer to think these are accidents.

I spy the cutest, tiniest little pineapple on a fruit stand. It looks ripe and so ready to eat. We buy it. Inside the store, I see the biggest cauliflowers, grapes, other fruits, and vegetables I have ever seen. It makes me want to cook! We move on. Damascus Gate comes into view.

A pretty dress stands out from among a collection of dresses hanging on the outside walls of a shop. This mauve colored dress has a Middle Eastern design down the front and on the sleeves. A pleasant young man greets us, "You want to see? Come." We follow him up the steep, narrow staircase where I sort of try one on. No dressing room exists, so he helps me put it on over my clothing while David watches. Even over a sweat shirt and pants, it seems large.

"It's too big," I say.

"Madam," he replies, and produces a size smaller and helps me pull it over my head.

"This one is too big, too." I am so hot.

"Madam, this one fits. You are skinny, but..."

"Oh, you do know what to say, but it's hot," smiling, I feel perspiration moistening my upper lip.

"This dress is not hot," he replies, "the very lightest material. It could be for a wedding."

"Yes, it's for a wedding" I agree.

"It's for the mother of the bride," he guesses.

"No, it's for the older sister of the bride."

I do like it. It's one of my favorite colors, but I know it will be warm in Kansas in June. I can wear it just for the wedding. Since it takes place in their home, I can change for the reception. This Bedouin dress seems more like a dress for the bride. In any case, I like it. And so the bargaining game begins.

"600 shekels, about $135," he announces.

Since 600 shekels is $150, David quickly changes to bargaining in dollars.

I object saying, "I cannot spend more for my dress than the bride spends on her dress, $100." David agrees.

"Look, I go $125," our salesman offers.

"I cannot spend more for my dress than the bride," I repeat.

He comes down to $110. After more discussion, he drops to $105. Then, finally he softens, "I like you. You take it. My gift to you, $100!"

I get my dress for the wedding. I love it! Like most Muslims we encounter, this man maintains a friendly and helpful attitude. As we leave he gently requests, "Please pray for peace."

Across the street, Damascus Gate looms in front of us. The area swarms with security. It looks like an officer's convention. The Israeli police in blue uniforms abound, decked out with riot gear, including helmets hanging from their belts. Numerous vendors busily set up tables with sheltering tarps outside the gate. Damascus Gate boasts the most elaborate gate of the Old City. The dramatic entrance of today stands over the remains of the original Roman gate. You can see the arch of that gate down low on the left as you approach crowded Damascus Gate. Perpetual motion and activity draws us, making it difficult to focus on anything. We stroll into the square just outside the gate. I spy something that looks like a delicious treat - layers of coconut and sesame under plastic wrap.

"What is it?" I ask the boy at the table. I point with my forefinger and touch the top of the plastic wrap.

"Madam! Do not touch the merchandise!" He nearly slaps my hand. I snatch my hand back for fear of losing it. "It is sesame, coconut, cashews and honey."

I must have it. You can't walk around and snack on this sticky treat, but one bite says "yum." I rewrap it and stick it in my bag.

We venture through Damascus Gate and watch more vendors set up. Something big seems about to happen, but exactly what, we don't know. We figure it involves lots more people and soon. In the meantime, we buy a couple of sodas, go back outside the gate, and find a good spot to people-watch. We have nearly an hour to people-watch, and I don't mind one bit. We find a pretty place, and sit on a stone fence separating the sidewalk from the grassy slope to the city wall. The place smells faintly like garbage. I try to ignore it. Sometimes my olfactory senses become far too efficient, so I concentrate on children playing down the hill behind us.

Boys playing near Damascus Gate.

A group of boys laugh and run. It sounds like lots of fun. The boys range from four to five years old. They play a fun game. One of them chases the others, holding something out at the others. Then he launches it at them. They run from it, laughing and shrieking. It hits the ground. One of the other boys goes over to pick it up for his turn. Now he can chase.

They're having a great time and I'm enjoying watching until I see what the boy picks up! A dead rat! He flings the dead rat at his friends. They run again, laughing hysterically. One of them comes back, picks up the dead rat, and the chasing begins all over again. I cringe. Every time one of those little boys picks up the dead rat, I call out, "No, don't do it. It's dirty." Whether they can hear me or understand me doesn't matter, they are having way too much fun!

God used this scene to remind me about our sin. God must look down and wince when He sees us pick up our dead rat (sin) again and again. Sometimes we think sin means having fun. Sin takes us further away from God than we ever intend. Sin distracts us in so many ways, yet we let it creep into our lives time and time again. One day we wake up and realize the dead rat we carry with us no longer makes any sense. We look with new knowledge and see clearly it holds nothing but danger. Thankfully, God can take away our desire to sin. As I contemplate this allegory, let me just say I don't want anything to do with my dead rat (or anybody else's for that matter).

An older boy, perhaps about 10 years old, sits on the stone wall not far from us. He pulls his hoodie up over his thick black hair. He has dark good looks of Arab descent. He sees me taking pictures, but I don't take any of him. He just sits there and keeps staring at me. Finally, I smile and say, "Hello."

"Hello," he answers.

"How are you?" I question.

"Fine," he says.

"Do you speak English?" I ask.

"One shekel," he says.

We get up to leave. Suddenly, hundreds of men come pouring out of Damascus Gate! Someone yells, "Friday prayers are over!" This explains the extra booths and vendors. We mix with the crowd expanding up the street away from the gate until we reach the turn to the entrance to the Garden Tomb.

A welcome respite from the hubbub outside, the Garden Tomb embraces the peace that surpasses understanding. Beautifully maintained gardens grace the landscape wherein lies an ancient tomb. It makes a wonderful place to sit and meditate on the Lord, who He is, and what He did for us. We love the Garden Tomb. Many Christians believe it is the place Jesus was laid and resurrected. Sadly, the archaeological evidence simply does not support it.

No one can prove the tomb belonging to Joseph of Arimathea, where Jesus' body laid, exists here. Speculation abounds. No one knows the location of the tomb of Jesus. This location meets some of the criteria, such as being near a skull shaped hill that may have been Golgotha (place of the skull). Solid proof doesn't exist. Fortunately, because Jesus sent the Holy Spirit, we can worship anywhere in spirit and truth!

Damascus Gate after prayers let out.

David asks the woman at the gate if we can have communion somewhere here in the compound. She shows us a quiet secluded place with marble benches and a short round table. A few minutes later, she brings us implements for communion. A rather large tour group comes in after us. I don't even notice them. They go to a different place in the garden. We pray. I read the Valley of Vision prayer David chooses:

O Lord,

In prayer I launch far out into the eternal world, and on that broad ocean my soul triumphs over all evils on the shores of mortality.

Time, with its gay amusements and cruel disappointments, never appears so inconsiderate as then.

In prayer I see myself as nothing; I find my heart going after thee with intensity, and long with vehement thirst to live to thee.

Blessed be the strong gales of the Spirit that speed me on my way to the New Jerusalem.

In prayer all things here below vanish, and nothing seems important but holiness of heart and the salvation of others.

In prayer all my worldly cares, fears, anxieties disappear, and are of as little significance as a puff of wind.

In prayer my soul inwardly exults with lively thoughts at what thou art doing for thy church, and I long that thou shouldest get thyself a great name from sinners returning to Zion.

In prayer I am lifted above the frowns and flatteries of life, and taste heavenly joys; entering into the eternal world.

I can give myself to thee with all my heart, to be thine for ever.

In prayer I can place all my concerns in thy hands, to be entirely at thy disposal, having no will or interest of my own.

In prayer I can intercede for my friends, ministers, sinners, the church, thy kingdom to come, with greatest freedom, ardent hopes, as a son to his father, as a lover to the beloved.

Help me to be all prayer and never to cease praying.[28]

28 Taken from *The Valley of Vision*, Banner of Truth Trust, Edinburgh, copyright 1975 Arthur Bennett. Used by permission. www.banneroftruth.co.uk

This appropriate prayer leads our communion service. David serves the bread and the cup as I read the familiar verses in 1 Corinthians, chapter 11, beginning with verse 23:

> *For I received from the Lord what I also passed on to you: The Lord Jesus, on the night he was betrayed, took bread, and when he had given thanks, he broke it and said, "This is my body, which is for you; do this in remembrance of me." In the same way, after supper He took the cup, saying, "This cup is the new covenant in my blood; do this, whenever you drink it, in remembrance of me. For whenever you eat this bread and drink this cup, you proclaim the Lord's death until he comes."*

Then God graces us with another little blessing. From another place in the garden we hear the tune to "Lord, I Lift Your Name on High," sung in a foreign language neither of us could identify. The familiar notes underscore the unity of the people who come here. We relax, rejoice, and praise our Lord. This special time calms and renews our souls.

From time to time, noise from the Arab bus station next door distracts from prayer. Suspicious, especially in unfamiliar circumstances, I presume Muslims honk their horns and squeal their tires to take away from the worship going on here. The Muslim presence becomes obvious when the 4:15 p.m. call to prayer fills this area via huge loudspeakers. An interruption now and then can be tolerated when you have the luxury of spending an entire afternoon here. However, if you happen to be with a tour group, you may have only 30 minutes. Tour guides avoid 4:15 p.m. and other predictable interruptions.

At closing time we stop by the gift shop. David finds journals to match the one he got at Moriah Bookstore and a couple of pens. I find the olive wood Christmas decorations I want, plus an olive wood thimble. The woman checking us out calls this day the quietest they have had since the Pope left in 1999, and the intifada broke out. That remark explains a couple of things. One, the number of security forces at Damascus Gate. And two, when the man at the dress store said good-by, he solemnly said, "Please pray for peace." At the time we assured him we always pray for the peace of Jerusalem.

We exit the Garden Tomb to find Sammy, the olive wood dealer, selling carvings from the boot (trunk) of his car. I met Sammy ten years ago. Mom and I bought olive wood camels from him. Sammy has been selling olive wood carvings from the trunk of his car at the Garden Tomb since 1969! He invites us to delve into the trunk and inspect his merchandise casually while we chat. He is an older man nowadays, likable, and perhaps in his late 50s. He has a family and lives in the West Bank. Sammy tells us his life became more difficult when the Israelis built the wall.

On June 16, 2002, Israelis began the construction of a separation wall to protect citizens from suicide bombers, weapons, and explosives from outside. Upon anticipated completion in 2010, this barrier will be around 400 miles long and 25 feet high. A great deal of controversy revolves around this wall. Palestinians must pass through checkpoints to go to work in parts of the country. Sammy must take a long route through a checkpoint, which adds to the inconvenience of the enormous traffic problems. Israeli Prime Minister Benjamin Netanyahu considers the wall in the West Bank area a critical component of his country's security. Despite the opposition, the controversial fence stays. Less violence occurred in the past few years because the wall exists. We buy two beautiful olive wood candlesticks and a carved camel from Sammy. I love camels, from a distance, from farther than spitting distance!

Our street slopes toward the Damascus Gate. Instead of entering, we walk outside the city gates to New Gate in the Christian Quarter. This way we avoid the souk. We already shopped enough. The walk leads uphill all the way.

Here's a picture of ancient versus modern. Outside the Old City walls, we walk on cobblestone-like streets. Next to that runs new construction for light rail! Upon reaching New Gate, we see the Pizza place we tried before – Yerevon's! The young man is the only one working. David looks at the grilled chicken pizza again. I say, "Just order it with no olives," remembering what happened last time. "I'm going to get it right this time," David insists, so he orders the pizza on the menu with olives only on one side. The young man seems to understand. When the pizza arrives, it has olives only on one side, just as David ordered. The only problem is that the menu said *black olives* and there on my side of the pizza sit *green olives*! We laugh.

Taking the tiny back streets through the Christian Quarter, we arrive at the Gloria just before nightfall. In the distance I hear fireworks, I hope.

The Tenth Day

Ramparts

*"Walk about Zion, go around her, count her towers, consider well her **ramparts**, view her citadels, that you may tell of them to the next generation. For this God is our God forever and ever; He will be our guide even to the end" (Psalm 48:12-14).*

Today we walk the ramparts of the city of Jerusalem! This tops my list of things we must do in Jerusalem. I can hardly believe it's taken us ten days to get to it. Jerusalem overflows with tempting options every morning. In the Old City of Jerusalem, the ramparts walk follows the walkway along the top of the inside of those huge stone walls surrounding the city. Today means such a victory! Physically, I could not have attempted it until now. Today I overcome my fear and attack the ramparts.

"In that day this song will be sung in the land of Judah: We have a strong city; God makes salvation its walls and ramparts. Open the gates that the righteous nation may enter, the nation that keeps faith" (Isaiah 26:1-2).

Nine o'clock finds us standing in line at the Jaffa Gate entrance to the ramparts, behind a tour group of around twenty people. Considering the steep stone stairway, they should go first. Undaunted, David purchases our passes. We expect this rampart walk to be the most physically demanding day of our stay. My weak knees already shake in anticipation. A hot sun shines, mocking my courage. I remembered my hat. David carries lots of water and snacks. We both carry our canes. We plan to go slow, pacing ourselves.

Checking the map, David says "We can get off at New Gate if we're too tired. I hope we make it to Damascus Gate. It's got a fabulous view from the top. If we continue, the map shows stairs down at Herod's Gate, but restoration work may block that exit. Then at Stork Tower we turn and change direction. Stork Tower offers the best views yet, supposedly. The map shows no way of getting down from there. Finally, we must exit at Lion's Gate. I don't expect us to get that far."

Right now I'm thinking New Gate. Going through the turnstile I'm resolved, *no turning back.* Another set of steep steps stands unmoving in front of me. These steps measure almost normal height. Once at the top I rejoice! The ramparts walk stretches out before me! I look down at the modern plaza and shopping center we visited a few nights ago. Across the way, the misnamed Tower of David stands tall. The narrow walkway has handrails appearing from time to time on either side. Count me grateful, even though I sometimes need to carry my cane. One of former mayor, Teddy Kollek's, projects provided these precious railings. He also insisted on narrow slats for the safety of children. Today we don't encounter any children on the ramparts walk, but pass classrooms filled with enthusiastic students.

The stones we tramp on are sharp and rougher than the cobblestones on the street below. At our first stop the sign reads, "The walls of Jerusalem include 35 watchtowers, one half of which were never completed. The towers protruding outward from the wall provided defenders on the wall with a wide field of sight and fire. Each tower is 2 or 3 stories high. The ground floor served as stables and storerooms, the middle stories as soldiers' living quarters and the upper stories, as guardrooms." The first tower demands we climb a series of knee-high steps to the guardroom. After descending (glad we brought our canes and thanking God again for these handrails), I start looking up the path for a shady spot. Another tour group passes. It's fine with me. Let them pass. We will surely run into their exhausted, dead bodies before the day is over.

On my right we pass by the dining room of our hotel. I nearly miss it. I'm busy looking outside the walls. I turn around and look into the dining room. Every morning for the past ten days, we've looked out onto the ramparts and watched people walk by as we enjoyed breakfast. For a while, I'm holding on and looking over the wall. The going really doesn't seem too bad at this point. We pass New Gate and continue going around the Christian Quarter. Walking the ramparts seems to be the best way to travel through the Old City, high above noise and confusion. Near Damascus Gate the sign tells us: "During and after the War of Independence, the (Jordanian) Arab Legion built military positions on the wall, from which

David inspects the city from the ramparts walk.

Legionnaires sometimes shot into the Jewish-held New City. These positions were removed after the Six-Day War in 1967, except for the remains of one position, which were preserved as a memorial."

We cannot walk the ramparts without thinking of the snipers and the 1948 and 1967 wars. Looking through the slots and feeling the massive stones around us, we find ourselves amazed at the bravery of the men who retook Jerusalem without the benefit of carpet bombing or napalm. If you saw the movie *Gallipoli*, then you know when men go up against entrenched positions the cost can be very high and the outcome uncertain.

75

We stand at the Arab Legion Military position. I peek over the side and look at the street below. I recognize the place David bought my dress. Down the street I see the entrance to the Garden Tomb.

"Do you want to get off when we get to Damascus Gate?" David asks. So far we stopped a couple of times for breaks. The sun blazes. I reason I would rather walk over the busy Muslim Quarter than through it, so we push on, slower. Every so often a salamander runs across our path. Cute, they afford an excuse for stopping and taking pictures. I can see the caption on this one, "Salamanders walk the Old City walls with Vicki and David." Further along I spot yellow spring flowers growing out of the ancient stones of the wall.

Damascus Gate impresses me as the most beautiful of all the eight gates of the city. Situated on the northern road leading to Damascus, it displays the extraordinary beauty of Islamic architecture. The straight block design of the wall gives way to eastern style minaret formations, very artistic. Looking away from the wall, I get a great view of the Dome of the Rock. Not too far from Damascus Gate we come upon the narrowest set of steps ever. The four tall steps each measure less than a foot across. Once at the top, we get our reward. David spots it the same time I do "The hill of the skull – Golgotha!" Gordon's Golgotha, discovered by British General Charles Gordon toward the end of the 19th century, resembles a skull. Unfortunately, the archaeological evidence does not support this as the historical site of the crucifixion. Even with sophisticated research and dating tools we use today, mysteries remain. The hill resembles a skull. I can see that. Is it the site of the crucifixion? No one knows for sure, but from this vantage point my heart soars with Gordon's. This could be it.

The spot upon which we stand exposes the best view of this famous hill. We take lots of pictures. It reminds us of what happened two thousand years ago. Jesus gave Himself up to pay for our sin in order that we could have a relationship with Almighty God. We thank Him once again.

It's getting hotter. The stones hurt my feet. Some steps in the area are thigh high. Getting up and down these beauties takes patience and imagination. I keep thinking my physical therapist would be so impressed. I pray no bones slip out of place! Herod's Gate stands closed, just as David predicted. No getting off here. We may have a problem. I peek over the steps of the tower looking for some way to continue on the ramparts. Do we need to backtrack? Once we get to the top, locked iron gates block the obvious route.

"O.K., back to Damascus Gate," David says as he turns to go back down.

I'm curious. I see the path continuing in the distance. I just can't figure out how to get there. *There must be a way.* I climb to the top of the stone stairway and inspect the perimeter of the flat stone guardroom floor. Sure enough, concealed by optical illusion, a metal stairway exists on the back corner of the floor. We descend and continue on the path, always keeping an eye out for a shady spot to sit. David mentions that if we make it to the corner a fantastic view awaits us. I see the corner. Soon we ascend the corner tower – Stork Tower.

The black plaque with white letters affixed to the wall informs us, "The builders of Suleiman's Wall erected one of the finest and prominent towers of the wall at the northeastern corner of the Old City. It is known as Stork Tower. It has been suggested that this was the spot where Godfrey of Bouillon breached the wall of Jerusalem during the Crusader siege of 1099; his coat of arms featured a swan, and since the Arabic word denotes a swan or a stork – hence the name."

This view surpasses the others. We gaze at Mt. Scopus, Hebrew University, and the Kidron Valley with the ancient tombs. Inside the wall, we peer down at the famous Pool(s) of Bethesda and St. Anne's Church. After taking lots of pictures we continue. I *head* down a covered stairway and WHAP! "Oh," I grab my forehead. "David. Watch your head!" *People must have been shorter back in the day.* Next we wander by an empty lot acting as a local dump. Getting rid of trash in the Old City presents a problem. If you don't have a truck, what do you do with junk that doesn't fit in the trash can? What a sad waste of an empty lot. I'm guessing real estate here rivals any place on earth. Who wouldn't want to live in Jerusalem's Old City? Perhaps the owner needs permission to build from the Israeli government. Once granted, the owner could clean up the lot and build something.

We pass schools, neatly decorated patios, flowers, and vegetable gardens. From Stork Tower, we turn toward Lion's Gate, also known as St.

Stephen's Gate. It seems everything in Jerusalem wears at least two names. This gate makes the last exit on this side of the rampart's walk. I feel pretty good. We never intended to get this far, but we did! The path doesn't stop here. We trudge on, past Lion's Gate. Why? Because. We walk the Old City of Jerusalem. We walk the ramparts! A few hundred yards away an ancient stone wall blocks our path. David sets his camera for the victory picture. We hold our canes high. We made it! We touch the northern edge of Temple Mount. Looking down on the main Muslim entrance to Temple Mount, we bask in victory in the shade of the old stone wall.

Vicki and David, triumphant rampart walkers.

We backtrack to Lion's Gate in order to get down to the street. I stop and get some great shots of the Church of All Nations and the Russian Orthodox Church on the Mount of Olives. God warned Suleiman the Magnificent in a dream to rebuild walls around Jerusalem to protect its inhabitants or lions would devour him. When he built this gate, he included carved lions on them to record victory over his vision. More recently, Jewish soldiers liberated the Old City by charging through this gate in 1967 – the Six-Day War.

Getting down at Lion's Gate drops us in the center of a Muslim plaza. While Jaffa Gate and Damascus Gate provide friendly taxi stands, Lion's Gate does not. Exhausted, we find a friendly shopkeeper who gives us stools to sit on while we drink cold drinks we purchase from him. Suddenly, thousands of people pour out of the Dome of the Rock and Al-Aksa Mosque onto the streets. Women dressed in fine burkas, with children in tow, stop for ice cream bars or popsicles. Men carrying prayer mats surround us. They want cold drinks or ice cream bars. They just got out of church.

David looks for a taxi or a bus. Traffic blocks the street with cars facing each other head on. Horns honk. No one moves. People flow around hopelessly gridlocked cars. Meanwhile, a man carrying a larger than life camera attempts to take pictures of a young woman dressed in a beautiful burka. She obviously does not want her picture taken. She keeps covering her face. He is so rude. My temperature soars as my face flushes with righteous anger. I want to get up and smack him! He finally gets his picture, turns quickly, and slithers into the crowd like a snake. I feel violated for her.

The crowd begins to thin out. I realize soon I will be required to move. My sore feet and knees rebel at this thought. But no matter, we plod over to the plaza to buy some bread, cookies, and more of that sesame seed treat. A Muslim man shakes his finger at me because, although my hat covers my head, I wear pants. He speaks in a language I don't understand, but I know exactly what he says. I can't go on the Temple Mount. I know. Two armed Israeli police block the gate – frowning at me. Let's get out of here. The Gloria waits. We start our long unplanned walk up the famous Via Dolorosa. We start as far as you can get from the Gloria. Walking the Old City means two things – lots of stairs and no taxis.

From Lion's Gate, through the Muslim Quarter to the Christian Quarter, the familiar Via Dolorosa leads us toward the Gloria. The Via Dolorosa traditionally traces the last steps of Jesus. Six of the ten Stations of the Cross display the history of the Via Dolorosa. We go only part way on the street and won't pass all of them. We reserve The Church of the Holy Sepulcher, where the other four Stations of the Cross reside, for another day.

We pass the first Station of the Cross - where they beat and condemned Jesus. The traditional site of the Roman Fortress where this took place resides inside what is now a Muslim college, the Madrasa el-Omariyya. The marked station demands a time for reflection. We pass the second station of the cross where Jesus takes up His cross. This station occupies the front of the Franciscan Monastery of the Flagellation. This Catholic Church complex includes the Franciscan Monastery of the Flagellation and the Church of the Condemnation and Imposition of the Cross. Walking farther, we pass under the Ecco Homo Arch, where Pontius Pilate uttered the words, "Behold, the man." The Convent Ecco Homo (Sister of Notre Dame De Sion) along with the Roman Catholic community provides a spectacular museum here. Barely off the hot, crowded street of yelling vendors attempting to sell their wares, this museum offers archaeological wonders and needed conveniences for the weary.

Once inside, a quiet, spacious, cool world awaits the battered and weary soul. Finding a deserted area, I sit. I begin looking around to explore my whereabouts. This museum houses some of the best preserved archaeological findings in Israel. Some items to see here include a cistern called the Struthion Pool, pavement with the ancient game of the king inscribed on it, and the famous arch built by Hadrian in 135AD. The convent's location may be just north of the place Herod's Antonia Fortress existed around 30BC. These archaeological remains helped archaeologist Leen Ritmeyer locate the original Temple Mount and the Holy of Holies. David takes the self-tour. I did it with Craig in 1998.

Clean rest rooms welcome me. They sparkle. After walking the ramparts in the heat of the day, I feel absolutely gritty. I wash my hands twice before going to the stall!

Upon his return, David remarks that in spite of his exhaustion, he found the museum tour immensely enjoyable and informative. The tour over, we step out onto the busy souk. A vendor motions us to his shop. He seems nice and not too pushy, so we go in. I find a green cotton dress and a couple of scarves. David keeps encouraging me to shop. I want to go to our little nest and rest. We leave this shop and find a clean, bright spot for a cold drink. I compliment the man on his shop. His uncluttered and bright coffee shop distinguishes itself from the rest of the souk. We trudge homeward the last few blocks of our trek. My clothes cling to me and they smell. Another, shorter, rampart walk around the other half of the city exists. It's in the plan, but not today, and not tomorrow.

THE ELEVENTH DAY

CHURCHES

"You will say then, 'Branches were broken off so that I could be grafted in.' Granted. But they were broken off because of unbelief, and you stand by faith. Do not be arrogant, but be afraid. For if God did not spare the natural branches, he will not spare you either" (Romans 11:19-21).

Craig and Renee celebrate their first year of marriage today. I email them a congratulatory note, after getting their answering machine earlier. My brother in law, Terry, celebrates his birthday today. We email and I call. My sister, Ginger, answers the phone. Her voice confirms her excitement at getting a call from Jerusalem. Ginger and Terry, committed Christians, love Jerusalem and the Land God gave to the Israelites. We wish Terry a "Happy Birthday." Ginger reminds us to keep safe.

For Sunday services we take the short walk over to Christ Church. Built in 1849, this elegant church proudly holds the title of the oldest Protestant church in Jerusalem. Strong believers in Romans 1:16, *"I am not ashamed of the gospel, because it is the power of God for the salvation of everyone who believes: first for the Jew, then for the Gentile,"* this church honors the Jews and our Hebrew roots.

The service begins with praise songs we know and then, to my delight and surprise, some Hebrew songs we sing back home! At home we sing the Shema to begin our service immediately after the blowing of the shofar.[29] The Shema declares, "Hear, Israel, the Lord is our God, the Lord is One. Blessed be the Name of His glorious kingdom forever and ever." The transliteration for the Hebrew goes like this, "Sh'ma Yis'ra'eil Adonai Eloheinu Adonai echad. Barukh sheim k'vod malkhuto l'olam va'ed."[30] I wish I could sing it for you. There are several websites that offer a musical rendition of the song. As we sing, I look around inside the church. High ceilings and archways in ancient-looking white stone brighten the sanctuary

29 A shofar is a horn made from a ram's horn.
30 Shema (listen or hear), Yisrael (Israel, in the sense of the people or congregation of Israel), Adonai (Lord), Elohenu (our God), Echad (one, as in the God is one).

Inside Christ Church.

The wall-sized stained glass window depicts a spectacular olive tree with a few branches broken off. This classic depiction of an aged olive tree reminds me of Scripture in Romans 11:17, *"... some of the branches have been broken off, and you, though a wild olive shoot, have been grafted in among the others and now share in the nourishing sap from the olive root..."* I am a wild olive shoot. This verse speaks to me just as much as it spoke to the Gentiles back in the first century.

The stained glass displays a Hebrew inscription. The Christ Church brochure translates those picturesque Hebrew letters as Scripture from Romans 11:29-31 *"For God's gifts and his call are irrevocable. Just as you who were at one time disobedient to God have now received mercy as a result of their disobedience, so they too have now become disobedient in order that they too may now receive mercy as a result of God's mercy to you."* "They, too," refers to the Jews. Shamefully, Jews often receive more hatred than mercy from Christians. Jews have even been labeled "Christ-killers." Hitler used the phrase to justify his own agendas. This thinking cuts me to the core. Hidden among the branches of the olive tree in the stained glass I notice both the cross and the menorah.

As a youth, I learned in Sunday school that Christians are the chosen people, replacing the Jews of the Old Testament. Now I understand more about the Scriptures and about how God works. First of all, God chose the Jewish people as His own chosen people. When they made mistakes, He used those mistakes to educate them and the rest of humanity. Through God's gift of faith, they remain His chosen people. In Deuteronomy 4:20, Moses tells the Hebrew people what God told him earlier, *"But as for you, the Lord took you and brought you out of the iron-smelting furnace, out of Egypt, to be the people of his inheritance, as you now are."* God could have said He would use them as a teaching tool for the world for a time and disown them for people who accept His one and only Son, Jesus. Instead, the Bible repeatedly affirms God's love and plans for the Jews.

The New Testament confirms Jewish followers of Christ before and after His crucifixion. The Gospels, written by Jewish eyewitnesses of His life on earth and His crucifixion, clearly illustrate Jesus had many Jewish followers. Even on the Temple Mount, His many Jewish followers congregated, so many in fact that the Pharisees feared arresting Him. *"The teachers of the law and the chief priests looked for a way to arrest him immediately, because they knew he had spoken this parable against them. But they were afraid of the people"* (Luke 20:19). The Jewish people loved Christ. The higher-ups, the political muckety-mucks decided to wait until Passover. Then, the Jewish people would be home celebrating Erev Shabbat.

We could say the Romans killed Christ. The truth is, neither the Romans nor the Jews could kill Christ if it had not been God's plan. No one took Christ's life. He laid it down for mankind. That means He **gave** His life for me, for the Jew and for the Gentile. *"The reason my Father loves me is that I lay down my life – only to take it up again. No one takes it from me, but I lay it down of my own accord"* (John 10:17-18).

A packed house at Christ Church soaks up a meaningful sermon in English. The communion service follows the message and begins with a congregational reading of praises. It lifts my heart. We sing the Shema a cappella. The congregation sounds like angels in the perfect acoustics of the old stone church. Tears of pure joy leak from my eyes. We read a confession together in unison and the Pastor reads an assurance of forgiveness. We repeat the Nicene Creed and another responsive reading.

The pastor gives an invitation to come forward and receive communion. As I kneel at the altar, he places a piece of matza in my hand, presses his thumb down, shattering the matza in my palm, saying, "This is my body, broken for you." I feel the matza snap into pieces. What a powerful demonstration of the Lord's suffering for us.

Another young pastor steps forward and offers a drink from the silver chalice he holds. "This is my blood shed for you," he ministers. I drink from the common cup and …another surprise – it is *wine*! I've attended lots of different churches, but none served the common cup. I'm proud of myself for trusting God enough to drink out of the same cup everyone else does, considering the flu pandemic going on at this time.

Afterward, a woman from London strikes up a conversation. David goes to take pictures I've requested while she and I chat. A retired school teacher, she lived in Israel seven years, four of which she spent volunteering at Christ Church. She went back to London years ago. She now seeks what the Lord would have her do. We agree to have tea later. I pose for David. In the flash it takes to record my presence in Christ Church, she disappears. Oh well, I thought she had an interesting story. Maybe we will run into each other again.

Back at the Gloria we rest, write, and enjoy the day. At 3:30p.m., we prepare to go to Kings of Kings Church, where a friend from back home presently attends. It's in the newer city of Jerusalem, in Davidica Square, down Jaffa Road away from the Old City. The taxi drops us in front of a tall office building. We enter past security guards. They don't seem to know about a church in the building. We venture downstairs searching for a sign.

Suddenly out of the blue, David says, "This looks familiar." *What? We've never been here.* "On the internet, I've seen this part of the building. We are in the right place, sort of." The elevator takes us to a lower basement. We enter a door looking more like it might be a restaurant than a church. At the front desk we register. We go down another floor to the sanctuary. The music team practices before the service. Since we arrive early, we get to listen. Loud! I would definitely say this church music's volume surpasses any I have ever heard. My ears adjust. We settle in to enjoy the practice. A couple of women in their 60s sit in front of us. When the praise service starts, they get up and begin to dance. Their joy lifts my spirits as I watch them dancing to the Lord. Even though loud, the music sounds great. Our friend slips in to take the seat beside me.

The sermon outshines the music. Young and energetic, the dynamic pastor delivers a memorable message about endurance. He recently ran what he calls a mini-triathlon, and parallels our race in this life to his experience. One point he made stuck in my head. He said resolve is good. Resolve will get you started, but endurance will get you there. Endurance is the key. Yes, I believe the message. I can't begin to count the number of projects I've started enthusiastically and didn't finish. My resolve faded before endurance kicked in.

Immediately after the service, our friend goes upstairs to the prayer tower. She prays with people for healing. They call it the "Healing Pools" ministry. David and I look at each other for a minute. We decide we could use some healing prayers. The Healing Pools occupies the fourteenth floor. Lots of people wait. We are last in line. It's all right because others have more urgent needs. No available seats remain in the main waiting area, so we find seats off to the side.

The man at the keyboard plays soothing hymns and sings. Every so often, he speaks softly, quoting Scripture. He continues playing. A woman sits next to the keyboard reading Bible verses softly. They switch back and forth. This blessed, precious time refreshes us. I relax and pray. I feel the presence of God in this place. Over one and a half hours pass before they call our name. We came for prayer. Both of us reluctantly leave the peace of the Healing Pools waiting room.

A lady ushers us into a tiny room. Another lady (one of the ladies that sat in front of us during the service) and a man pray for our healing. We talk about our maladies for several minutes, maybe half an hour. Then they anoint our heads with oil, lay hands on us, and pray for us individually. The experience blesses us. At 9:30 p.m., we snag a taxi back to the Gloria. Five and one-half hours at King of Kings! What unspeakable joy to spend the day with God and His people.

THE TWELFTH DAY

ARCHAEOLOGICAL PARK

"Jesus left the temple and was walking away when his disciples came up to him to call his attention to its buildings. 'Do you see all these things?' he asked. 'I tell you the truth, not one stone here will be left on another; every one will be thrown down'" (Matthew 24:1-2).

We eat protein bars. I fix my tasty International Coffee in our room for breakfast. We want to leave before the dining room opens. As hot as it has been during the day, an early day at the archaeological park works best. I dig my dirty clothes out of our makeshift hamper. The clothes I wore on the rampart walk will do nicely. They already stink!

We begin thinking like the locals in some ways. We've discovered getting around goes faster if you walk outside and around the city walls. We exit Jaffa Gate and turn toward the route I walked back in 1998 to Jerusalem University College on Mount Zion. Traipsing down the hills, memory kicks in for my knees. They begin to hurt. I start feeling sort of, well, not good. We cross the tricky intersection and start up the hill toward David's Tomb. Oh, yeah, here it comes - diarrhea. The bathroom inside the building at David's Tomb remains locked at this early hour. We already walked down to the school and back up to the vacant lot where ten years ago our professor, Wink Thompson, lectured us about the sandstorm in which we stood. David and I come in the back way by Dormition Abbey, but too early for open bathrooms. We continue around the city walls to Zion Gate. We get to Zion Gate and the usually not so clean public rest rooms. Yea! This time they have paper. My condition comes on as a result of the heat. Sometimes my body reacts this way. I admit, and David will agree, I've been cranky since our start this morning. I keep praying for God to change my attitude. I feel angry. I keep kvetching like an Israeli in the wilderness, all the time asking for forgiveness, knowing what a gift it is to even be here. Yet, I continue focusing on my suffering until reaching the Temple Mount. Soon after arriving at the archaeological park, God grants me rest from myself. Once again, I concentrate on His work and His plan that centers on Yeshua and Jerusalem.

The Jerusalem Archaeological Park reveals amazing discoveries about Jerusalem during the Second Temple period. Resting on the original steps Jesus walked to enter the Temple Mount at the Hulda Gates overwhelms. We admire the southern wall of the Temple Mount in the area known as the Ophel. These bleached stones reflect the summer heat. David snaps a few pictures. I make my way back to the shade-providing awning. Sitting here, I notice men working on top of the Al-Aksa mosque. They swelter in this heat, and I sympathize with them.

Vicki and David stand before the Hulda Gates.

In the meantime, David falls in love again. All the things he read about or saw on the net live here; the trumpeting stone, the Temple mikvah, the huge broken stones of the temple tossed off the Temple Mount by the Roman soldiers in 70AD, the Herodian street with the shop doorways on the side, and so much more. David returns from his short tour on the west side of the Temple Mount excited. He witnessed a group of junior high school aged youths on a field trip. They sing loud and clear, "Ki MiZion, tetsay Torah...."(The law will go out from Zion). He recognizes it because we sing it every Shabbat before reading from the Torah. We consider this special moment a divine appointment. David feels another connection to

Jews living in Israel today. Their love of Torah reminds him of the depth and riches of Christ he missed before reading the Old Testament.

Archaeological findings reveal a history fueling my imagination. Perfectly honed Herodian streets with distinctly carved stones tell the story of wealth and riches. Stones on the ground that fell during the destruction of the Temple - the smallest of which weighed two and one half tons - report the devastation of war! An unearthed Byzantine home unwraps mysteries about everyday life centuries ago. The mikvah declares the past presence of priests and devout men. Across from my shaded awning I see the remains of the Umayyad Palace from the early Islamic period and a huge impressive tower built by Fatimad Sultan, renovated by the Crusaders, the Ayyubids, and the Mamluks. Even today, God draws people from all nations to this small spot. The heat of the day beats down on us.

Out on the plaza soldiers, in groups of thirty or more, walk by. Some groups carry large automatic rifles, others show none. These young men and women always catch my attention. They hold the task of protecting this incredible country. While sitting under the awning, I see a hundred or more of them pass toward the southern wall of the Temple Mount. Across the way, but still under the awning, three women and a man sit sharing a stone bench. Another man (obviously a guide) talks about the significance of this place. The group looks absolutely exhausted. The man in the bright orange shirt looks like he may fall off his perch any minute. One woman just looks bored. The other two women question the guide repeatedly, prolonging the agony of the man in the orange shirt. Poor fellow. David and I drench our thirst, then our faces, necks, arms and clothes in the drinking fountain and amble over to the Davidson Center.

The Davidson Center ranks high on my list of favorite or most dramatic surprises. The center explains the archaeological findings just outside using a range of exhibits. *The Story of the Pilgrim*, a movie at the center, inspires me. It includes a virtual view of what Solomon's Temple probably looked like. We walk into the little theater while the Hebrew movie with no subtitles is still running. We sit through the Hebrew version for fun. We want to see how much Hebrew we can understand. Can we pick up the story line? Some words we recognize and figure we know what goes on most of the time. I begin feeling a little smug about getting the language. Then the English version starts.

Well, we got some of it. Most of it we totally miss, including the main plot. I love *The Story of the Pilgrim* about a man who comes from far away to worship at the Temple. It cost him a year's wages and several weeks to make the journey. When he sees the splendor of the Temple and goes to make his sacrifice, he is humbled. This virtual reality model captures the grandeur of the Temple much better than scale models. The Temple looms majestically, although not as majestic as the One it honors. I am humbled by His very presence within me.

Outside again, loud music, singing, and chanting come from the upper plaza near the security gates. A band plays. I hear familiar Hebrew songs flowing from the plaza. Loud drums beat and children sing. As they get off yellow school buses, the music stops. Shofars sound. Then we hear more shouting and music. Excitement fills the air! Most of the three hours we spend at the Jerusalem Archaeological Park includes hearing this assemblage. We finally get up to the plaza and encounter a Bar-Mitzvah parade! They celebrate bar-mitzvah for boys (bat-mitzvah for girls[31]) on Mondays, Thursdays, and Saturdays. When a Jewish boy reaches the age of 13 (12 for girls), friends and family join in the special birthday celebration. That's when they reach the age of religious duty and responsibility.[32] It encompasses more, but you have the basic idea.

Since David heard Christ Church serves a good lunch, we hike up the hill for a nice spot on the patio. A quiet refreshing place with shade branches overhead welcomes us. The pastor who preached Sunday's sermon sits near us. He did a great teaching on how God cannot be coerced or manipulated. Unfortunately, we often find ourselves doing just that more often than we like to admit. A tour group comes by. I recognize one of the ladies as the song leader last Sunday morning. Last Sunday, the pastor introduced a young couple with a newborn to the congregation. They intern here for a year before moving on. Relaxing on the patio brings all this and more flooding back to my mind.

---

31 Very orthodox Jews, such as the Chassidim, do not observe the American practice of a bat mitzvah for girls.
32 Under Jewish Law, there is no obligation for children to observe the commandments (mitzvot) before the age of 13 (for boys) or 12 (for girls), although they are encouraged to do so. After the age of 13 or 12, they are required to observe the commandments. A boy, after his age of bar mitzvah, can now be considered as part of a minyan.

After lunch I make an executive decision. On this hot day I will do best spending the rest of the day at the Gloria. My knees still hurt from our fun day on the ramparts. David, eager to see more of the Old City, goes exploring. Thankfully, I get busy reading and writing. Out of curiosity, I switch on TV. Yes, we have TV in our room. We've been here two weeks and never had it on. I can't get it to work and call the office. They send a man who shows me what button to push. How embarrassing. He leaves. I push the magic button. Headlines fill the screen, "Netanyahu meets with President Obama" from the BBC! I turn it off.

David returns to the Jewish Quarter and gets the Scripture for inside our mezuzah from the Scribe, Yosef. He also buys a beautiful painting. Beautiful, but expensive, so he considers it his special souvenir of our trip.

He visits two museums. Although quite old, Rabbi Wiengarten, the spiritual head of the Jews, got unjustly hauled off as an exile to Jordan in 1948. After the reunification in 1967, his daughters and others created the *Old Yishuv Court Museum* as a visual testimony to the fact that Jews lived in the Quarter before 1948. It displays Jewish rooms during various periods before 1948.

Alone on the Ramparts museum shows pictures and film of the battles for independence in 1948. The sad movie causes David to wander the Cardo area aimlessly for awhile lost in his thoughts. David comes back to the Gloria totally wiped out. To cheer him, I remind him of Israel's national anthem, HaTikva (The Hope). *"In the Jewish heart a Jewish spirit still sings and the eyes look east toward Zion. Our hope is not lost, our hope of two thousand years to be a free nation in our land, in the land of Zion and Jerusalem."* We googled HaTikva and listened to a beautiful version by Barbara Streisand voicing the resiliency of the Jewish people and the faithfulness of their God.

I fix him a chocolate shake with peanut butter. Fixing a shake is a lot different here than back home. I start with lukewarm tap water (disguised under the cold-water faucet), add chocolate protein shake mix, and powdered peanut butter. Then I use David's battery powered whisk. What I don't end up wearing, he gets to drink! In the Old City of Jerusalem, you never get ice for a drink. They just hand you the bottle or can of soda. If you ask for a glass with ice, they reply, "It's cold." However, David gets ice from the hotel bar almost every night for his knee. I feel positively naughty by using some of the ice in a Pepsi Max. Oh, but it's such a treat!

Bread stands and all kinds of food sellers abound in the Old City. Bread arrives daily along with food served in all the restaurants. Tourists purchase bottled water and souvenirs that must be restocked. Shockingly, loading docks do not exist here. Yesterday I saw a flat bed truck delivering a full load of bottled water to the Western Wall, probably a standard daily delivery. Everything here costs because of the expense of getting things in and out. Trucks can navigate only a few streets, so pushcarts must do the work. A small tractor pulls the hand loaded trash cart along the steep streets.

The amount of inventory these little shops hold amazes me. Each little hole in the wall holds tons of products. Stuff stacked from floor to ceiling – necklaces, bracelets, earrings, bric-a-brac (whatever that is), rocks, wood carvings, silver, coins, and more overflow into the street. Things that don't sell just stay. They never go away. Once they become antiques someone will buy them.

THE THIRTEENTH DAY

ZEDEKIAH'S CAVE

"The Lord said to him [Solomon]: 'I have heard the prayer and plea you have made before me; I have consecrated this temple, which you have built, by putting my Name there forever. My eyes and my heart will always be there'" (I Kings 9:3).

This morning we breakfast in the dining room. The granola cereal I've become fond of, a sweet roll, coffee, and eggs makes for a good start today. The people at the table across from us have been here all week. He wears a bright orange shirt. It occurs to me the poor, exhausted fellow we saw at the archaeological park had the same shirt. The lady sitting next to him looks familiar as well. Goodness! Our breakfast neighbors roasted under the direction of their guide yesterday.

I lean over saying, "Didn't I see you yesterday at the Davidson Center?

One woman says "no."

The other woman says, "oh, yes, the archaeological park! I'm wearing the same clothes."

There's a lot of that going on in Israel. They came from a suburb of Detroit, Michigan. The younger lady, on a tour three years ago, brought a small group of seven back with her. The group leader tells us they hoped for a group of thirty, but they enjoy a great tour as a smaller group. We make small talk for a few minutes. They go to Petra tomorrow.

The older lady says, "Tell me the truth. How hard is it and is it worth going up to the monastery?"

What I remember about Petra she doesn't want to know. I tell her she should plan to pace herself. What can I tell her about her threshold for pain versus her desires? One person might not give a fig about a monastery carved out of a granite rock, while another might be inspired by it.

David has a busy day planned. He aims to hoof it over to Damascus Gate to explore the ancient gate below the present one. Then he plans on seeing Solomon's Quarry and Zedekiah's cave. I tell him his adventure sounds fun, but I have seen them before. I will see him later. I do the laundry, read some, check the computer (no emails), and write. I relax and reflect on all the things we've done since we arrived almost two weeks ago.

Meantime, David takes the back streets to see more of the city, especially peoples' residences. A lot of old men sit around and look bored with nothing to do in the Old City. Clerks sit outside a shop waiting for customers. Often they just sit, and perhaps smoke. Jerusalem must be a tough place to be old. Summer heat combines with many stairs making getting around arduous. Everything is expensive.

David stops at Murad's shop to see the tallit clip he ordered. Murad made good progress on it. He introduces David to Johnny, his brother, and they chat a little. Johnny tells David about a place that may have the camel leather belts he desires. David finds them not yet open at 10:10 a.m. Some souk shops have opened; some remain closed at this early hour. Ten a.m. to eight p.m. are normal hours, but if they don't like those hours, they open later. He heads out for Damascus Gate via back streets. He hopes to see local shops instead of tourist shops. Turns out, he sees more apartments than shops. Offices, grocery stores, toy stores, an arcade with very old arcade games, among other things line the streets. These streets meander with corners, but David stays oriented and ends up in the souk of Damascus Gate, one block from the gate.

Elderly ladies sit on the ground selling green leaves. Perhaps they grew them. He buys a bunch of mint leaves for two shekels (about 50¢). It looks like a quart of them. When I wash the leaves and spread them out on a towel, it looks more like a bushel. I hope the mint helps the water.

One enters the Roman Plaza Museum and archaeological site through the old Damascus Gate. They uncovered the gate, dug out the debris and dirt from around the walls, and worked on restoring Damascus Gate after the 1967 War. Inside the old gate they discovered an old Herodian street, from the time of Christ. Jesus probably walked where David walks today! The towers and storage rooms uncovered from various periods reveal a wealth of interesting artifacts. It cannot be moved to a museum because it supports part of the current gate structure. These two remarkable sites do not draw many tourists. David passes through the Damascus Gate from the time of Jesus and onto the street. Alone, he walks with Jesus along the 2,000-year old paving stones.

Archaeologist Charles Warren believed Solomon quarried stone from Zedekiah's Cave for the Temple. Later, Herod expanded the quarry as he enlarged the Temple. Either way, the cave looms enormous, the size of three football fields end to end, all underneath the old city.

Zedekiah's Cave is huge.

People say the quarry sits uphill from the Temple. It does. Getting the stones out of the quarry required moving them up a steep uphill grade before gravity becomes your friend moving them downhill. No one mentions that part of the job. Rock removed from the original small cave created this current massive cave. It takes half an hour to descend to see the last place active quarrying took place. David examines channels cut where they put in wood and soaked it or whatever they did to break out a finished square for the Temple. The astonishing size surprises David. Such a huge space sits unused under the crowded City. It smells okay. Considering its possible past uses, it must have been a major undertaking to clean out the debris and build steps. David appreciates the lighting. He stands alone down here, carrying a tiny flashlight in case of a power failure.

David returns at 1:00 p.m. promptly for our lunch date. I so appreciate his promptness. Rossini's Restaurant across the street served the Pope.

We have high expectations. The mahogany bar and matching furniture speak quality. Brocade tablecloths with matching napkins announce, "*This is going to cost you a few shekels.*" David orders lamb. It comes in a fancy presentation with ribs sticking up in the air. I choose filet mignon with heavenly mushroom sauce. The waiter speaks good, but broken, English. We mention seeing their sign last week that they served the Pope.

"It was my great honor to pour wine for the Pope," beams the young man. David asks what the Pope drank. "He drank orange juice." We smile, enjoying the insider information. At twenty-one years old, our waiter fulfilled his lifetime dream. I wonder what one does after achieving one's lifetime dream at such a young age.

He presents a dessert menu – my weakness. David suggests hot chocolate mousse with vanilla ice cream. Not wanting to hurt his feelings, I gleefully accept his suggestion. The vanilla ice cream tastes out of this world, the best ever. The hot chocolate mousse touches the divine. I can't hide my delight. We stay at Rossini's for quite awhile. At 3:30 p.m. we leave after a two and half hour, 300 shekel (about $75) lunch.

We narrow our choices of what to do tomorrow down to two: the 99-bus tour of the city or an archaeological dig in another part of the city. Both of these options mean leaving the Old City. Both seem interesting. On the 99-bus tour, we can get off and on at different interesting sites. An archaeological dig appeals to me. It's something I've always wanted to do. We delayed *dig day* because of the recent hot days. Someone told David earlier the heat wave ended yesterday.

Then I hear David talking on the phone to someone about reservations for a trip to Hebron in a bullet-proof bus! Okay. That gets my attention. We couldn't go to Hebron back in 1998. The largest city in the West Bank, Hebron numbers over 160,000 Palestinians with less than 1,000 Jews. Located in Judea, called the West Bank by the rest of the world, Hebron holds a revered place in the hearts of Christians and Jews. The name West Bank irritates me. Why don't they call it what it is – Judea and Samaria. King David ruled the first seven years of his monarchy from Hebron. The second holiest site in Israel, after Jerusalem, the Cave of the Patriarchs, Abraham, Isaac, and Jacob lie in Hebron. My heart skips a beat when David schedules us to leave in the morning! The bus leaves at 9:15 a.m. from Sheraton Square downtown.

I am so blessed, so *very* blessed. I thank God every day for David. David takes such good care of me. Right now, he charges my camera battery and replaces the chip with a new one. I will have plenty of pictures and not have to worry about running out of battery or memory while on our tour of Hebron. David is my hero. We will be at a holy site. I dig out the cotton dress David got me at the souk. Without jeans and shirt underneath it hangs loose. I must remember to wear a head covering.

David makes me talk with the lady who took our reservations, "Is it safe?"

"Of course it is safe. We have many soldiers to protect us." I feel assured, but forget to ask why the bullet proof bus. She didn't say there wouldn't be any shooting.

The mint helps the water. I add stevia. Excellent! Thoughts of Cynthia run through my mind. I've emailed and spoken to Ginger. I'll call and see how the wedding plans go. She's at work, so I dial her there.

Finally, "This is Cynthia."

"Greetings from Jerusalem; how are you?" She's surprised.

I hear her say to someone nearby, "It's from Jerusalem!"

She's busy getting ready for her wedding and her only worry now concerns getting everything done before the wedding. She and (her) Dave will get married whether everything is done or not. We have a great conversation and both admit we miss talking to each other. Back in the states, we talk almost every day. We start to hang up. She says, "Be safe."

Oh, I couldn't help myself, "Well, we are going to Hebron in a bullet proof bus tomorrow. But they say it's perfectly safe." Now why did I have to say that? It sounds dangerous. She knows I'm not brave. If the tour endangered lives, they wouldn't go, with or without a bullet proof bus. On the other hand, Hebron is West Bank territory. Most people believe it's not safe for anyone but Palestinians. In 1998 and 1999, Hebron topped the list of places not to go. The reference to a bullet-proof bus emphasizes the lack of confidence tour arrangers have in the present political situation. They don't know the future any more than I do. Currently, tour buses travel safely to Hebron without any shooting.

David went to get laundry we sent out this morning. Because everything is so expensive in the Old City, we cut down where we can. We only sent the really stinky clothes from the ramparts walk and the archaeological park. I washed the rest. He picks up ice for his knee. It's nice of him to share ice, since I beat him at cards earlier tonight.

I make iced mint tea with vanilla stevia. I'm ready for bed. The Hebrew lessons on my iPod put me to sleep. I should sleep well, even though excited about tomorrow's adventure.

THE FOURTEENTH DAY

HEBRON

"So Ephron's field in Machpelah near Mamre – both the field and the cave in it, and all the trees within the borders of the field – was deeded to Abraham as his property in the presence of all the Hitites who had come to the gate of the city" (Genesis 23:17).

We wake early. Breakfast consists of two boiled eggs, toasted buns with honey, and something very good and sweet. A group from Boulder, Colorado shares our dining room this morning. Their tour group, organized by Peace for Palestine, goes to the West Bank today, too. We live near Boulder. It feels like our snooty, snobbish neighbors showed up. One lady out of the entire group makes conversation. She happens to be from Colorado Springs, the only one not a Boulderite. The others discuss ways to solve the Middle East's problems.

We finish breakfast, pack up our gear, and go directly to the taxi stand at Jaffa Square. The driver says 40 shekels to Sheraton Plaza. Sarah said it was a short walk, but uphill. We mentioned we would be using canes. She didn't amend her suggestion. It may be a short walk for her, but not for us. We arrive first. Sarah smiles, clutching a clip board, "You must be the Andrees."

"How did you know?"

"You both carry canes!"

O.K., so we're not famous.

Our guide, Sarah, lives in the newest Jewish community right across a small valley (Shepherd's Field) from Bethlehem. Interestingly enough, Sarah reveals she does not like the security wall. This special tour by the Hebron Fund helps support Jewish families and Jewish neighborhoods in Hebron. Very few Jews live in Hebron. Jews live here at considerable risk. They stay to maintain Jewish access to Abraham's Tomb.

People begin filling the bus. It becomes obvious we booked a Jewish tour. Some look Orthodox, while others wear modern clothes. David wears his white shirt and black pants. I wear the dress I picked out yesterday with a beige scarf. Two of the families on board have come to Jerusalem from some other country to celebrate their children's bar and bat mitzvahs. We feel honored to sit among them. We find seats at the very front, behind the driver.

Our bus begins leaving the parking lot. Sarah starts her introduction to the tour. Our driver makes a left turn to squeak by a sherut (minivan taxi). Well, the sherut screams. Our bus makes a deep crease in its side, toward the back. Sarah doesn't notice it happened. She keeps talking. The sherut driver calmly gets out of his vehicle and observes the damage. Meanwhile, our driver backs up, parks the bus, and gets out to talk to the Sherut driver. Sarah still talks. She hasn't missed a beat. I'm cracking up. She is oblivious to what happened.

Finally she says, "I don't know what the hold up is here," turning around to look out the windshield, "but it looks like there's been some sort of accident." Then another man comes up to talk with the two drivers. That's when Sarah says, "I'd better go see if we can get moving. When three Israelis ..."

She doesn't finish her sentence, but we get the drift. Soon everyone gets back on the bus. Our old bullet-proof bus looks the same as any other bus on the street. The narrow seats feel comfortable. A Jewish couple sits across from us. She stands up and uses the bus rear view mirror to put her make up on right in front of everybody! Her husband, with long beard and Orthodox dress, looks older. She sits down just before our first stop.

"So Rachel died and was buried on the way to Ephrath (that is, Bethlehem). Over her tomb Jacob set up a pillar, and to this day that pillar marks Rachel's tomb" (Genesis 35:19-20). Rachel's Tomb comes into view, our first stop. In 1998 we could not go to Rachel's tomb. We drove past it several times, but never stopped. The school considered it too dangerous to visit. Since then, the Israelis built corridors to and from the tomb. These corridors tower over 20 feet high and border both sides of the street. They surround the site of the tomb. The bus must pass through a security checkpoint before steel gates open allowing entrance to the parking area. Once inside the building we undergo another security check. Then we can view Rachel's tomb.

This Jewish tour allows at least half an hour to pray at each important site. For most on the tour, including ourselves, that's the highlight of the tour. Sarah knows we are Christians (the only ones on this tour) because yesterday David slipped and said "Pentecost," instead of "Shavuot" when talking about our schedule. His wedding ring displays an obvious cross. We are not ashamed of the gospel, but we try not to offend others.

The men enter the viewing room on one side, and the women, out of sight from the men, enter on the other side. As I enter the women's side, I pull my scarf over my head as a gesture of respect. The Jewish women pray with their prayer books. Some rock back and forth like men do at the Western Wall. I sit quietly in a corner and contemplate Rachel's life. Jacob fell in love with her. I think she fell in love with him. He worked seven years for the right to marry her. I wonder what Rachel thought during those seven years. Her older sister, Leah, did not marry during the time Jacob worked for Rachel. By tradition, Rachel's older sister had to be married first.

Jacob wanted to marry now. Laban, Leah, and Rachel hatched a plan. It must have been the only workable solution at the time. Rachel tricked Jacob into marrying Leah first. What kind of woman goes for a deal like that? Rachel must have been absolutely confident of Jacob's love for her. Jacob loved Rachel more than he loved Leah. Rachel birthed his two favorite sons, Joseph and Benjamin. The Tomb of Rachel stands over the traditional place Rachel died, giving birth to Benjamin. According to geographical descriptions related in Scripture (Genesis, 1 Samuel and Jeremiah), this cannot be the correct historical site. Yet this is where we traditionally honor her. Rachel died at a young age. I sit here in front of her tomb feeling sad for her. Rachel didn't get to raise her baby sons or see her oldest in the seat of power in Egypt. She missed so much.

Many people journey to Rachel's Tomb because she brings inspiration to women and mothers. She raised a godly child, Joseph. David prays and thanks God for Rachel and Joseph, a type of Christ. He also thanks the Lord for his own godly mother, Josephine.

A tiny old lady sits in the chair next to me. I recognize her as the lady asking for alms when we first came in the building. I ignored her then, hardened by people asking for shekels or trying to force us to go into their shops in the Old City. Now I feel the Lord drawing me to her. My Spirit tells me to give her something. *But, Lord,* I think, *I only have 20 shekel bills.* I hear Him say in my heart, *so.*

I slip the folded bill into her tiny hand. She smiles and gives me a red string. I don't know what this means. I don't know what to do with it. We sit in a quiet and sacred place. She doesn't speak English. Talking can't happen. I can tell by her smile and sparkling eyes, it means something good. She takes the string and ties it around my wrist, then blows me a kiss and kisses my hand. She keeps patting my hand, then, gives me another red string. She mouths some unrecognizable words and gestures. She wants me to give the other string to David.

Out in the hall I ask our guide about the lady. Sarah reminds me that since Biblical times the government has allowed the poor to ask for alms in certain holy sites. In return for those alms they bless you. The red string tells everyone you have received their blessing for peace and good luck. More importantly, it reminds the wearer of God's generous nature and the blessings they received from Him enabling them to share with others. A woman standing near me says, "Look, my mother gave me one before she died." She holds up her wrist. She shows a silver bracelet with red string running through it. I tie the other string around David's wrist.

We board our bullet-proof bus, go through the heavily armed and guarded checkpoint, and turn toward Hebron. The road to Hebron takes us through the hills of Judea. Before we get there, we must pass the Palestinian city of Bethlehem. In 1998 and 1999, I got to go to Bethlehem. Both times I went to Nativity Square and the Church of the Nativity. Later, in April, 2002, Palestinian gunmen took over the church and held hostages for 38 days. Seven Palestinians died in the confrontation. Because of this history, and the Hamas presence, guides tell us not to travel in Bethlehem. The Israelis solved the problem of traveling through Bethlehem by building a tunnel under the city. We go underground and come out into the Judean hillside. A carpet of green covers hills dotted with fruit trees and vineyards. Ancient rock retaining walls support terraced fields. Some of the world's finest wines come out of these vineyards. You can probably buy it at your local liquor store. The countryside gives way to concrete walls, for safety's sake. These walls suddenly disappear as we roll down a steep incline, through a narrow street, into Hebron.

Inside the small building a soldier signals our checkpoint. This checkpoint seems quiet now and not very rigorous. We can tell that in troubled times it could revive quickly. Now soldiers get more serious about checking loads on trucks headed into Jerusalem.

The bus stops on a narrow hillside. Our guide for Hebron boards the bus. Rabbi Simcha Hachbaum begins by giving us a little background of the Jewish settlers. This community began in 1984 with seven trailers that had to be set up within one 24-hour period. These trailers look worse than any we see in our communities back home. A waiting list exists to live in one of these old trailers. We stand in the Tel Hebron Admot Ishai neighborhood. The 63 year-old great grandson of the First Chief Rabbi got murdered in one of these trailers. To console the widow, then Prime Minister Netanyahu released permits to build new homes. The Jews raised money and constructed apartments for eight families. Later, the nearest Arab neighbor wearied of snipers hitting the wrong house and sold out to a NYC consortium of Hebron supporters. Today, only eighteen families live in this settlement.

Rabbi Hachbaum gets out of the bus. We follow him up the hill along paths fortified by soldiers and guarded on either side by 20-foot metal fences. Finally we stand in a children's play park. This small Jewish school, surrounded by a few apartments, became one of several Jewish settlements in Hebron. They live here hoping to take back their city. Their faith sustains them as they wait for God to accomplish their impossible dream.

The Biblical site of Hebron, founded some 3,700 years ago, became the first dwelling place of Abraham in the Land. Our guide keeps saying ancient Hebron belongs to the Jews. Abraham purchased it at full market price. The Jews have a record of the event, Genesis 23:7-9, *"Then Abraham rose and bowed down before the people of the land, the Hittites. He said to them, 'If you are willing to let me bury my dead, then listen to me and intercede with Ephron the son of Zohar on my behalf so he will sell me the cave of Machpelah, which belongs to him and is at the end of his field. Ask him to sell it to me for the full price as a burial site among you.'"* He paid the full market price of 400 shekels for the two caves, which the guide tells us equals the full market price today, $1.5 million. He bought both the field and the caves in it. Genesis 23:16 seals the deal when Abraham pays the price.

Rabbi Hachbaum takes us from the fledgling Jewish school to a small cave at the top of the hill. I'm embarrassed when he points out the resting place of Jesse, the father of King David. The rough concrete bears a blue spray painted Star of David (Magen David in Hebrew). It's far from the respected place one would expect. In fact, it's a bit trashy around the site. Ruth, the Moabite, King David's great grandmother rests here, too! An entire book in the Bible relates her story of loyalty to the Hebrew people. Here she lies in a rather unkempt place in Hebron. Unkempt, but revered by all who come to pray and pay their respects to these honored ancestors.

The rabbi gives a Torah lesson worthy of our Torah teacher, Daniel. He tells us that because Ruth was a Moabite, she was required to obey the Seven Laws of Noah.[33] The Hebrew name Ruth has a numerical value of 606. By changing her name to Ruth, she proclaimed that when she said, "Your people will be my people and your G-d will be my G-d," she took on the additional 606 laws of Moses. 7+606=613. The Jews teach 613 commandments (mitzvot) to live by as recorded throughout Torah and rabbinic teaching.

Next, a couple wants to light a candle at the tomb. Rabbi Hachbaum tells them to pray in whatever tradition brings them closer to G-d. This rabbi is a true encouragement to everyone.

In the Jewish Quarter of Hebron, Spanish exiles flourished until 1929. In August, 1929, riots broke out. Residents suffered torture and murder from their Arab neighbors. The British deported the innocent survivors. In 1948, the Arabs completely destroyed the Jewish Quarter and built a wholesale market, a trash dump, and a public toilet on the land. An animal pen stood over the previous site of the Avraham Avinu Synagogue. In 1967, newly liberated Hebron commenced restoration of the Jewish Quarter. It was slow going. In 1976, the government ordered evacuation of the animal pen, enabling the remnants of the synagogue to be uncovered. By 1989, settlers restored the Avraham Avinu Synagogue.

---

33 The Noahide Laws (The Seven Laws of Noah) are a set of seven moral obligations given by God to Noah as a binding set of laws for mankind. The seven laws are You shall not ...have any idols before God, murder, steal, commit adultery, commit blasphemy, or eat animal flesh while the animal is still alive. Mankind must have just laws governing their people.

In the Sephardic[34] Synagogue next to his apartment, Rabbi Hachbaum tells an inspiring story about the desertion of the synagogue in 1936. The British drove the Jews out of Hebron. A young man grabbed the ancient Torah scroll that had originally been rescued from the Spanish Inquisition. The founders of this synagogue brought the scroll to Hebron. When the Brits kicked them out, the young man vowed to bring it back when Jews returned to Hebron. At age 83, he did. Rabbi Hachbaum opens the Ark and lets us see that very Torah scroll. The Bar Mitzvah and Bat Mitzvah children come forward to examine God's faithfulness. After this, the rabbi graciously invites our group into his own apartment.

Arabs don't allow Jews in Arab parts of the city, including most stores. Down the hill on the way back to the bus, we see a sign, "This land was stolen from the Jewish people in 1929." This faded, beat up, red and white sign has some rust on it, confirming age. In 1929, Hebron's Jewish population suffered a horrible massacre. Shocking photographs in a small museum reveal gruesome details too disturbing to relate here. We board our bus again, not missing the sight of soldiers everywhere.

We soon arrive at the Cave of Machpelah, the final burial place of the fathers of our faith, Abraham, Isaac, and Jacob! The Cave of Machpelah reveals the site of a 3,700-year-old real estate deal between Abraham and Zohar, the Hittite. Two thousand years ago, Herod built the building that stands over the caves. What a history this building has, being conquered time and again, and reused for different purposes. The Byzantines and Crusaders used it for a church. The Muslims considered it a mosque. Seven hundred years ago the Mamelukes forbad any Jew beyond the seventh step on the staircase outside the building. The building, run by the Muslim Waqf (religious trust), restricts Jews. In 1994, an unfair agreement gave Muslims most of the area, including the Isaac Hall. Isaac Hall, the largest hall, leads down to the caves themselves. How ironic. Muslims don't recognize Isaac as the *chosen* and only son of Abraham and Sarah. They recognize Ishmael born to Abram before God changed his name to Abraham. Ishmael's body doesn't reside in these tombs. Jews can enter that part of the building only ten days a year. Many of our group choose to pray at the wall outside the building, nearer the actual cave Abraham bought.

---

34 Sephardic Jews originate from the Iberian Peninsula. Ashkenazi Jews originate from the Rhineland, and represent 80% of the world's Jews.

Praying at the wall nearest the cave Abraham bought.

We climb around 120 steps, just getting into the building from the street. This impressive piece of architecture exhibits Herod's building skills. The tombs inside the building imitate the real tombs buried beneath the building. The fake tombs stand behind thick bars decorated with a heavy coat of peeling green paint. The fake tombs themselves look about twelve feet tall under a decorative green, carpet-like shroud covered with a coat of dust. The thick coat of dust marks them as ancient.

We see Abraham's tomb, Sarah's tomb, Jacob's tomb, and Leah's tomb. All the time I sense Isaac and Rebekah's presence as well. Each tomb reserves a place for prayer, divided for men and women. Some people pray with heads bowed or from prayer books. Museums in the Old City look cleaner, yet somehow less holy. I focus on these patriarchs and their wives. What do they mean to me, a Christian here with a Jewish tour? Abraham stands out as the honored father of our faith. Sarah, as an old woman, becomes a first-time mother through faith. Jacob responds to God and changed from selfish to selfless. Leah, the woman who raised Rachel's baby, Benjamin, helped Jacob mourn for the loss of his beloved Rachel. Yes, Leah, the woman who stood by Jacob for the rest of her life. I take pictures of all the tombs and the different signs in Hebrew with their names on them. I reflect on the story of Isaac and Rebekah and all our leaders of the faith. I thank God for each of them and praise Him for the work He did in them so we can know Him better and believe. I thank the Lord for bringing me here to pay homage to these that He chose. I feel so unworthy. Walking back down the steps to the bus we see more soldiers, reminding us of the security screening we went through just to enter the building. We board the bus and turn toward Jerusalem.

The bus drops us off across from the Great Synagogue in Jerusalem. We peek in the door. A man says they are closing. The room we peek in is huge and very impressive. Back on the street, we figure if we round the corner, we can get a taxi. Looking up, we encounter the famous Moses Montefiore windmill. Erected in 1857, this mill ground grain into flour, but only for a short time. The Israelis used it as an observation point during the War of Independence. It's now a restaurant, but everything looks closed, so we go back on the street. This time a taxi picks us up right away. He whisks us back to Jaffa Gate. It's been a long day. I forget my camera in the back seat of the taxi. All of my pictures of Hebron vanish along with the pretty pink camera David recently got me. No matter, I could not forget today even if I tried.

THE FIFTEENTH DAY

DIG DAY

"For there is nothing hidden that will not be disclosed, and nothing concealed that will not be known or brought out into the open" (Luke 8:17).

David arranged for us to go on an archaeological dig today. His knee aches this morning. The long line at the buffet surprises us. George, one of the wait staff, comes by with coffee.

George smiles excitedly, "We serve 180 people this morning."

I snag a couple of boiled eggs, rolls, and the sweet loaf I now enjoy in spite of its looks. Avoiding the line for hot food, David grabs an orange. He decides to fix a shake back in the room. One little Japanese lady nearly knocks me down. I accidentally got between her and the tofu yogurt, or something equally disgusting. The room fills with noise and excitement as everyone fuels up for their adventures today.

Back at the room we decide to travel light. David's knee hurts badly. He asks if I will carry my own chair. No problem. These are the lightest folding chairs ever. I can do this. Out the door, we limp down the hill to taxi square. We talk with several drivers searching for one who knows how to get to our destination. After a big powwow, they decide one will drive. The other will sit in back with me and give directions. He takes us on back streets through the Old City to the Kotel. Here, the man in the back seat gets out and gives change to another driver. We got to run an errand! Then we head out of the Old City to our destination.

After traveling down a dusty dirt road we arrive at piles of rubble and a big tent. Always thinking ahead, David writes down the driver's cell phone number. We need a driver who knows how to get here when we finish. We anticipate a fun day.

We arrive at Tzurim National Park ready to work. The site looks interesting. The trainer introduces herself and begins telling us a fantastic story. When the Islamic Waqf dug out the area known as Solomon's stables, they removed a lot of old rubble. They did this excavation with bulldozers (instead of teaspoons). The Islamic Waqf doesn't give a fig about Jewish artifacts or Biblical archaeology. Eager to open a new prayer area, they excavated under the Temple Mount just like any construction site in the United States. Israel requires archaeologists to investigate and preserve a site before construction begins. Incredibly, the Islamic Waqf ordered the debris disposed of in the local dump!

The construction took place under the ancient supporting arches of the Temple Mount built by King Herod. When Herod rebuilt the Temple to extend the Temple Mount, he more than likely used debris from the First Temple, Solomon's Temple, for landfill. An enterprising young archaeologist began digging in these dumps. He found some very interesting items. Someone complained. The police arrested him. He ended up in court. The police confiscated his finds and turned them over to the Minister of Antiquities. The court ruled he could legally work the dumps. Anything he finds belongs to the Ministry of Antiquities. Since then, he found this place to store the piles of dumped trash. People like us pay to sift through it! What a concept. Today we join archaeology students in the only Temple Mount dig since the days of Charles Warren. The Temple Mount Antiquities Salvage Operation began in November 2004, established by Dr. Gabriel Barkay, who found the silver scroll in 1979, and Zachi Zweig. Three hundred truckloads of topsoil from the Temple Mount must be sifted. Where do we begin?

Archaeology fascinates me. Biblical archaeology, in particular, gets me pondering about episodes of the past. Knowing more about places and objects discussed in Scripture helps me better understand God's message. The Biblical archaeology accomplished in the last century staggers my imagination even more than recent space exploration. These physical objects often illuminate Scripture and vanquish doubts. The first time I toured Caesarea, Dr. Wink Thompson, our professor at Jerusalem University College, pointed out a copy of a limestone block with the name Pontius Pilate on it. This ancient limestone block proves Pontius Pilate existed. Other than the Bible, the only information written about Pilate came from two Jewish historians, Josephus and Philo. Christ's death sentence by Pontius Pilate led to His crucifixion. Before this major archaeological discovery, some theologians doubted the existence of the man who remains unmentioned in the surviving Roman records from that time. Evidently, Jewish historians, for whatever reason, were not considered reliable sources. Later, our group went to the Israel Museum in Jerusalem and saw the original piece, discovered at Caesarea in 1961 by an Italian group of archeologists led by Dr. Antonio Frova.

Another top archaeological find we discussed on Day Five/The Silver Scroll. These silver scrolls (the largest one about four inches by one inch) found tightly rolled up into two small amulets, rocked the scientific community. This find is considered the oldest Scripture found yet.

The oldest New Testament text found consists of a scrap of papyrus from the Gospel of John, discovered in 1920 in Egypt. The Dead Sea Scrolls, found in 1948, proved our Bible's accuracy. In 1975, an Arab East Jerusalem merchant produced the Seal of Baruch, additional evidence of the Bible's accuracy. Baruch served as a scribe to Jeremiah the prophet, *"Instead, the king commanded Jerhameel, a son of the king, Seraiah son of Azriel and Shelemiah son of Abdeel to arrest Baruch the scribe and Jeremiah the prophet. But the Lord had hidden them"* (Jeremiah 36:26).

The discoveries constantly underlining the truth of Scripture bless us. Believers in the past had the Torah, the Old Testament, and the New Testament. For many, no other evidence seemed necessary. In the days Jesus walked the earth, believers saw and believed. Jesus blessed Thomas when he needed to see the scars in Jesus' resurrected body to believe. Then Jesus said those who believe without seeing receive even more blessing. We don't see those scars on Jesus' body, but today we see evidence of the past, confirming what we already believe written in the Word. God strengthens my faith through archaeology. Strong faith withstands the devil's lies.

As recently as 1994, the Basalt Stelae, found in Dan, confirms without a doubt King David existed. Theologians and critics rejected accounts of King David, Israel's beloved King, for centuries. This find contained the words, "house of David," the first external evidence of his existence. Once again, archeology supports the accuracy of Scripture. Workers discovered the true site of the Pool of Siloam in 2004, as they dug to repair a sewer pipe. Jesus sent a blind man to wash and be healed in this pool near Hezekiah's Tunnel. Christians hold in highest regard these incredible discoveries unearthed in recent years. David and I don't expect to find anything newsworthy. The idea of finding even a few pottery shards from ancient times sounds like an adventure! In this project, the archaeologists classify and statistically track each shard of pottery or glass from each period.

Our trainer instructs us on how to properly find artifacts. We look for at least six different things: pottery, metal, bones, mosaic tiles, glass, and special rocks. The special rocks constitute anything marble. Any marble found here comes from the Temple. About 50 buckets of debris covered with water sit in the center of the long canvas tent. First you choose a bucket. Then you dump the contents on a screen, being careful to wash out the bucket. Good things tend to stick to the bottom. You spread debris over the screen and power-spray it. You turn them over and spray them again. Now the fun begins!

Our trainer assigns us an expert for additional on the job training and supervision. Moran, our expert, checks our screen after we think we found everything. The first bucket yields pottery chards, some Byzantine tiles, a piece or two of glass, some metal pieces, and bone. We spend half an hour working this screen. Moran checks and finds some pottery chards and a few tiles we missed. David takes a snapshot of our valuable finds. Like kids in a candy store, we eagerly grab another bucket. This time we carefully recheck everything so when Moran comes, he won't find anything. We do get better, but Moran always finds something. At one point, Moran thinks he finds a coin. He gets very excited.

"This is a big find," he says, "I've been doing this for three years and I've never found a coin before." He runs into the main building to confer with the boss. She comes back with great fanfare. She struts around the building displaying the coin on a special paper plate for all to see!

The coin find fires us up! We look even more intently. We find mosaic tiles with gold on one side, one with bright blue glaze on it, and an ancient one from the Dome of the Rock. Moran identifies that one immediately. We find Herodian, Byzantine, and Roman tiles, Roman glass, and a spine bone. I enjoy finding the Byzantine tiles. They appear square, the color of Jerusalem stone, and comparatively heavy. Tiles soon become my specialty, but I want to find a coin. David finds two ancient nails. Sporting an impish grin, he tells me they came out of Jesus' sandals. These one and half inch nails might work on platform sandals. I never find any metal. Moran reminds me bones are significant. They could be bones of animals used for sacrifice at the Temple. I play up Moran's earlier extraordinary find by teasing him and pretending to find another coin.

Around noon we take a break. I don't want to stop. Another group is on the way and our trainers want us to wait for them. We've been the only volunteers here all morning. Being the center of attention of the archaeologists and salvage personnel maintains our focus and entertains us. We sit back and wait for the new group to join us. Soon a school group marches into the area. They stop by our screens to watch us work. Amused at their curiosity, we pretend we know what we're doing. Everyone wears blue and white. Many carry Israeli flags. Jerusalem Day is tomorrow but, because of Shabbat, they celebrate today.

After lunch snacks we start sifting debris again. David spots a glazed blue tile about the size of my hand! A great find!

I pick up a thin, black piece of asphalt with metal and tell Moran, "This is my coin."

He laughs, and then looks serious. "Yes, it looks like a coin," he hurries into main building where the expert's expert works.

"Yes," he returns excited, "It is a coin. It is a good find!" He congratulates me. Later I feel sad. His coin turns out to be just another piece of metal.

Another archaeologist cleans up my coin. They allow David to take pictures. Then they tag it, placing it in a plastic sleeve. The archaeologist promises that if it turns out to be a rare coin, they will email us. Certificates proving we worked on their project materialize. We leave feeling more knowledgeable about archeology than when we arrived.

The taxi lets us off at Jaffa Gate. Earlier, one of the drivers told us we should go to the visitor information center to get some help finding my camera. The man at the information center tells us to take the short walk up the street to the police station. Up the hill, across from the citadel, the police are in the process of changing shifts. Officers on horseback ride into the compound. One horse sweats foam. I cannot imagine how hard it is for a horse to navigate these cobblestones. We go through security into the confusing compound. A guard directs us to the first door on the right. We have hope because I remember the driver's name.

I find a coin in the Temple Mount debris.

Using his computer, an officer searches the traffic ticket database for Schlomo Schneiderman in the estimated age bracket. He makes a few phone calls. I hear him say, "Yofi, yofi!" I recognize "Yofi" from conversational Hebrew classes two years ago. "Yofi" means "splendid" in English. I assume good news. He hangs up the phone. I lean forward expectantly.

"Sorry, Ma'am, none of the Schneidermans listed drive taxis." If anyone turns in a camera, they will contact us. Caught off guard, I forget to ask what is so splendid. The officer suggests we call 144, get a list of all the taxi companies in Jerusalem, then call to ask if they found a camera. He insists our hotel will help us. We will try that after a little rest.

THE SIXTEENTH DAY

JERUSALEM DAY

"Jerusalem is built like a city that is closely compacted together. That is where the tribes go up, the tribes of the Lord, to praise the name of the Lord according to the statute given to Israel. There the thrones for judgment stand, the thrones of the house of David" (Psalms 122:3-5).

Jerusalem Day commemorates the victory of the 1967 Six-Day War and the reunification of Jerusalem under Israeli control. This minor religious holiday celebrates a Jewish Jerusalem. Jerusalem is all about the Jewish people and the God of Abraham, Isaac, and Jacob. In 1948, Israel's announced independence met with attacks from her Arab neighbors. The Jordanians took over the Old City and east Jerusalem. Immediately they forced out all Jewish residents. Arabs destroyed most of the fifty-eight synagogues. They looted Jewish tombstones on the Mount of Olives, and used them for paving stones and building materials. Even more demeaning, the territory in the vicinity of the Western Wall became a public dump. For years, the sporadic battle between the Jordanians and Israeli Defense Forces continued. It took a major war to recapture the Old City.

Those who fell in battle during the six-day war fought valiantly. This day memorializes them. On June 11, 1967, a cease-fire ended the war. On May 12, 1968, the government declared Jerusalem Day a holiday. It took 30 years, until 1998, for the Knesset to officially recognize it as a national holiday. Since Jerusalem Day is celebrated on the 28th of Iyar on the Hebrew calendar, the date changes every year on my calendar. Memorial services along with services in synagogues thank the Lord for reestablishing Jerusalem as the center of Jewish worship.

Moshe Dayan's famous speech below supports recognition of Jerusalem Day.

"This morning, the Israel Defense Forces liberated Jerusalem. We have united Jerusalem, the divided capital of Israel. We have returned to the holiest of our holy places, never to part from it again. To our

Arab neighbors we extend, also at this hour— our hand in peace. And to our Christian and Muslim fellow citizens, we solemnly promise full religious freedom and rights. We did not come to Jerusalem for the sake of other peoples' holy places, and not to interfere with the adherents of other faiths, but in order to safeguard its entirety, and to live there together with others, in unity.

Young Israeli student carries his flag on Jerusalem Day.

Last night, about 10:30, we heard fireworks like the Fourth of July. The sky above the Citadel lit up. This morning, church bells ringing joined birds singing to wake us. Bells ring from several different churches about every two hours. Today I plan to kick back, rest, review pictures, write, and pack away things we don't currently use. David's swollen knee needs ice. I want him to give it a chance to heal. We go up for breakfast late. Most of the crowd is gone. A quiet breakfast, looking out at the ramparts, sets the perfect pace for today.

At noon, I go out for two loaves of our favorite sesame bread and two Pepsi Max drinks. The crusty, chewy Arab sesame bread reminds me of a huge soft pretzel with sesame seeds instead of salt. Upon my return, I call all the taxi companies in Jerusalem, but get no help on the missing camera. The lady at the front desk says she made some calls and no one can help. There is no more I can do. I give it to the Lord.

Shabbat begins at sundown today. Beginning this Friday evening until sundown Saturday evening, Jews will spend their time resting and being with their families and other Jews. Considered the best day of the week by Jews, we celebrate it back home, as do others in our congregation. The fourth commandment states *"Remember the Sabbath and keep it holy."* God created the heavens and earth and everything in them in six days. On the seventh day He rested. God created the Sabbath for man to rest and remember what He did. Everyone can relate to how busy we get during the week. For instance, here we are on *vacation*, yet every day we do something to increase our knowledge of Jerusalem and the Jewish people. We push to satisfy our yearning to understand more about our faith through our Hebraic roots. At home in Colorado, every day means work, chores, and responsibilities. Often we fall into bed exhausted at the end of a day. God didn't fall into bed exhausted. Why did He rest on the seventh day? I think He paused to enjoy His creation and fellowship with Adam. He is our example. "Shabbat" literally means rest. Shabbat rest means forgetting the pressures of life for a day and enjoying time with God and friends.

Raised in Protestant churches, neither David nor I had any exposure to Shabbat until the last few years. My first encounter with Shabbat happened in Jerusalem in 1998. Craig and I shopped at Moshe and Dov Kempinski's shop, Shorashim, in the Old City. Moshe, who is always open to conversation, taught us how to say, "Shabbat Shalom!"

"It means 'Have a peaceful Sabbath,'" Moshe translated. "The Sabbath is our holy day of the week."

That day I purchased a refrigerator magnet with the words "Shabbat Shalom." It remains on my office file cabinet eleven years later. It reminds me of the kindness and patience of Moshe that day as he spoke of many things concerning his faith. He calmly indulged us by answering question after question about the Land and his religion. Whenever I look at these words on the file cabinet, I'm standing back in that little shop with Moshe teaching me to say "Shabbat Shalom!"

God planted a seed in my heart those days in Israel. I noticed, as all visitors soon find, Shabbat strictly observed (more by some than others) in Jewish neighborhoods. This observance set the Jews apart from other people. God desires His people be set apart from the rest of the world. By observing Shabbat, Jews honor God. A few years later, I began to get convicted about the Fourth Commandment, *"Remember the Sabbath and keep it holy."* I asked myself what that meant. Holy means set apart. As believers in Christ, we become set apart, different from the world by the way we think, act, and believe. As a child, I remember businesses closed on Sundays. If traveling, you needed to fill up Saturday night because gas stations closed on Sunday. Most American Christians observed Sunday as a holy day. No one grocery shopped. Restaurants closed. Most businesses shut down for the day. After church, families spent the day together. We loved to go for a Sunday drive in the country or work a big puzzle together. Historically in the United States, Blue Laws were enacted to enforce religious observance on Sundays. Today, Blue Laws have been ruled unconstitutional. How sad!

It took some time to get my mind around Shabbat and worshipping on Saturday. It happened slowly. Worshipping on Saturday seemed foreign. Knowing Jesus went to church on Saturday, I wanted to join Him. Eventually David and I found a congregation worshipping on Shabbat, celebrating the same feasts and laws as our Lord and Savior, Jesus Christ. Now every Saturday friends welcome us to congregation with warm smiles and the words, "Shabbat Shalom."

Is observing Shabbat and other feasts mentioned in the first five books of the Bible legalistic? Nothing could be further from the truth. My freedom through my relationship with Jesus Christ allows me to celebrate the feasts and explore my Hebraic roots. I strengthen that relationship by engaging in activities Jesus did while on earth. As I participate in the feasts, I grasp more about Jesus and His relationship with the Father. I become acquainted with the desires of the Lord. The feasts demonstrate what God wants for me and what He wants from me. They underscore what He has already done for me and what He intends for my future.

Given by God, Shabbat begins on Friday night. It's a family affair. Everyone gets in on the preparation. In Jerusalem, I saw men stopping by flower stands on their way home from work, picking up flowers for the occasion. His wife spent the day cleaning, shopping, and preparing food for the special meal served tonight. She sees that the food for the next day remains accessible.[35] After doing most all her chores, she dresses up for the onset of Shabbat. Shabbat is valued as *queen* of the week. Traditionally, in many Jewish households the song L'Cha Dodi (Come My Beloved) is sung on Shabbat to welcome the Shabbat Queen. If the Queen came to your home, how would you dress? Your dress, home, food, and attitude would be your best.

At precisely eighteen minutes before sundown, the woman of the house covers her head in reverence to the Lord and lights the Shabbat candles. Then she covers her eyes and prays the Hebrew blessing[36] over Shabbat. I could find no reference in the Old Testament commanding us to light candles. For many Shabbats I changed the prayer to bless the Lord God as King of the universe, who commands us to honor the Sabbath. In time, I came to realize the lighting of the candles meant we honored the Sabbath.

Now I pray the traditional prayer. Then we bless the wine[37] and thank God for the fruit of the vine. After saying the blessing, we take a sip, clink our glasses together, and say, "L'Chaim" (to life). After that, we bless the

---

35 Observant Jews maintain special requirements during Shabbat. They must not start or stop a fire, drive a car, turn off or on lights, cook, write, carry things in the street, do things that require work or physical exertion, use electricity, or buy or sell things. Jewish women, when preparing the Shabbat Friday evening meal, will prepare enough food so that there are leftovers the following day, thus relieving them of having to cook/work/turn on electricity, which is forbidden on Shabbat. The leftover stew served on Saturday for lunch is called Cholent.

36 *Barukh atah Adonai Eloheinu, melekh ha'olam, ashcr kid'shanu b'mitzvotav v'tzivanu l'hadlik ner shel Shabbat.* Blessed are You, Lord our God, King of the universe, Who has made us holy (set apart) through His commandments and commanded us to kindle the Sabbath light.

37 *Barukh atah Adonai, Elohaynu, melekh ha-olam, borei p'riy ha-gafen.* Blessed are You, Lord, our God, king of the universe who creates the fruit of the vine.

Lord for the bread[38] He brings forth from the earth. I love to bake the Challah (bread) instead of buying it. During the time of putting it together and braiding it, I meditate on the goodness of God. I thank Him for this special day of the week, as well as the many blessings he has poured out on us during the week. We pass the Challah. Each person tears off a piece. No knife is used. This is a time of peace. The meal officially begins.

It's Shabbat. I enjoy reading from the Bible sometime before the meal ends. Our Shabbat celebration involves less structure than most right now. It may never change. As Jesus said, *"The Sabbath was made for man, not man for the Sabbath"* (Mark 2:27). As time goes on, our Shabbats have and will continue to change. At the end of the meal I extinguish the candles as David prays the Aaronic Blessing, *"The Lord bless you and keep you, the Lord make his face shine upon you and be gracious unto you; the Lord turn his face toward you and give you peace"* (Numbers 6:24-26).

I love Shabbat. On Sabbath morning we attend services, followed by a congregational time of lunch and fellowship. At 2:00 p.m., we begin Torah study and midrash for two hours. Midrash means we study Torah and discuss the deeper meaning revealed by scholars and our own experiences. I have been a Christian for more than fifty years. I've read the Bible cover to cover many times. Yet every week I learn something new about a Scripture verse during Midrash.

Today we rest. I miss our Erev Shabbat at home, but we celebrate in spirit. For dinner I go across the street and pick up a falafel for David and a schnitzel for me. We dine out in our little courtyard. Afterwards, we play cards and I call friends and family to hear voices I've missed since we left. They all get excited about receiving a call from Jerusalem!

---

38 *Baruch ata Adonai, Elohenu melech haolam Ha-motzi lekhem min ha-aretz. Blessed* are You, Lord our God, King of the universe, Who brings forth bread from the Earth.

THE SEVENTEENTH DAY

SHABBAT

"Remember the Sabbath day by keeping it holy. Six days you shall labor and do all your work, but the seventh day is a Sabbath to the Lord your God. On it you shall not do any work, neither you, nor your son or daughter, nor your manservant or maidservant, nor your animals, nor the alien within your gates. For in six days the Lord made the heavens and the earth, the sea, and all that is in them, but he rested on the seventh day. Therefore the Lord blessed the Sabbath day and made it holy" (Exodus 20:8-11).

After resting yesterday, David wants to buy presents for friends filling in for him at work while he vacations. Shabbat in Jerusalem means shopping won't be done in the Jewish Quarter. People in the Jewish Quarter will be observing the Sabbath. Some of them spend today in worship and studying Torah. Shops in the Jewish Quarter shut down. No buses run today. No Jewish taxis run. God expects Jews to work hard during the rest of the week. Many Scriptures in Torah direct them to work hard, work faithfully, and work honestly. This one day they do no work. Orthodox Jews do not even cook on the Sabbath. Work provides tangible pleasures like food and heat. As physical and spiritual beings, we need spiritual food. Shabbat helps balance the spiritual and the physical worlds in which we live.

We turn toward the Christian Quarter. Shopkeepers here don't accost you like those near Jaffa Gate. One man perches in front of his door. His shop looks interesting. Some pretty dresses catch my eye. As far as I know, no dressing rooms exist in the Old City. I already own two dresses too big for me. I tried those on over my clothes. As much as I love the embroidery work on the front of these dresses, I resist temptation because I cannot tell what they would look like on me. David asks my opinion on a cute Druze bag for a female coworker. I approve. The man in the shop offers coffee. I shudder. Remembering the taste of Turkish coffee, I tell him, "Water, please." He presents me with coffee anyway, along with a small glass of water. The coffee proves me correct. As I expect, it tastes horrible. Grounds float on top and settle in the bottom of the tiny glass. I gulp it down, being polite. The water chases away the bad taste.

We move on to Murad's shop. Always happy to see us, they offer us seats and send out for orange juice. Murad finished David's tallit clips made with the small silver scrolls. The clip shines beautifully and the juice tastes delicious. I decide to buy gifts for some friends in our congregation. A twelve tribes pendant and a pendant with the menorah and sign of the fish on it catch my eye. These pieces have deep meaning for those of us grafted in. The twelve tribes came from Jacob, whom God renamed Israel. The twelve tribes represent the children of Israel. The menorah and fish memorialize the foundation of the Christian faith and the shared values of the Old and New Testaments.

At Murad's we find a bunch of old rusty keys. These keys once opened gates within the Old City. One of David's coworkers, who appreciates antiques, will receive a key with an appropriate Scripture. We pick through keys for a long time, being sure to get just the right ones. Murad shows off for us. He heats up Turkish coffee with a blow torch under a tin cup! They do like that coffee. Murad made me a special gift. I can tell it took some time and effort. He gold-plated and bezel set a modern 1/10 of a shekel pendant that shines brilliantly. A beautiful piece I will wear and treasure because he made it especially for me.

David wants to buy widow's mites for Christians covering for him at work. Murad tells us about a coin dealer who attends his church. Basically, he tells us the guy won't rip us off. Zak carries quality merchandise. Young, yet patient, he impresses us. David gets five sets of two widow's mites in excellent condition. Zak boxes them up and writes out certificates of authenticity.

The account of the widow's mite presented in the Gospels of Mark and Luke reminds us how we should give from the heart. In the Temple, Jesus watched people giving their tithe for the Temple treasury. Many rich people gave great amounts of money. Some made a huge show of what they gave. They enjoyed being the center of attention and impressing each other. A poor widow put two small coins in the till. Although worth only a fraction of a penny, Jesus commended her because she gave out of her poverty. The others gave out of their wealth. God loves a cheerful giver. He loves to see someone cheerfully sacrifice to please Him. Gifts given to impress others don't impress God. Given the story behind the widow's mites, these will be special gifts. The Hebrew word for charity is Tzedakah.[39]

Zak shows David first revolution (Maccabees) and second revolution (Bar Kochba) coins. I see David intrigued, but he says, "No." I can tell its not bargaining strategy. I still have to find a reproduction of a Roman glass tear bottle for a friend back home. I ask Zak where I should look for imitation glass. He happens to have the real thing! He makes us a good deal on it. The price far exceeds what my friend wants to pay for imitation. I suddenly become interested in this authentic piece. Zak's honesty and good salesmanship kicks in. He makes us an offer we can't refuse, which includes all the items. Yes! We happily buy all of it. I can hardly wait to get that little tear bottle on my antiquities shelf.

We have lots of fun with the good-natured fellow across the street from Zak's store. David wants some belts for our guys back home. The fun part is deciding who they will fit. I yell across the way at Zak, "You're about the size of my son. Come over here and see which belt will fit."

Being a good sport, Zak comes over. When the man tries to sell me a dress, he does everything but try it on himself! I keep telling him, "Too big!" He knows it and I know it and he knows I know it, but he keeps trying. He even runs down the street to another shop twice to find the right dress, but sorry, no sale. I leave empty handed, while David carries four new belts.

Leaving Murad's, we stop for lunch. Coincidentally, it turns out to be the shop of the man who brought us orange juice at Murad's. He makes a good lunch, chicken grilled with onions, salad and french fries! As we bow our heads and pray over our meal, his voice joins ours in "Amen." His little hole in the wall restaurant, named the Falafel Chapel, blesses us. A tile on the wall hallows the place, "May the Lord bless you as you enter the Falafel Chapel and bless you as you go out." Most people grab a falafel from the counter facing the street and move on. They either rush by or their tour keeps them moving. Sadly, most miss this encouraging blessing.

---

39 Although Hebrew word for charity is Tzedakah, it has an expanded meaning for Jews. It means righteousness, justice, fairness. Giving to the poor is not viewed as a generous, magnanimous act. It is the act of justice, giving the poor their due.

Back at the Gloria we prepare for the Night Spectacular at the Citadel. We need to grab a bite before we leave. We venture upstairs for the usually good and quick dinner buffet. Tonight they serve steak and potatoes! Good choice.

Across Jaffa Square, we arrive at the Citadel to see a new light show called *The Night Spectacular.* This amazing light show uses 45 projectors to throw dynamic scenes onto the ancient walls of the Citadel. The stone walls of the Citadel transform into various scenes of Jerusalem history, complete with live action and music. The artistic style for the background switches between magical and realistic throughout the presentation. Stone arches and trees appear. Animals and people walk through them. Your senses no long distinguish real walls from projected images. The story begins at creation. It depicts Jerusalem at the inner heart and center of the world. Scenes fly by, telling the story of Jerusalem and its people. When we see the majestic Temple in flames, tears fill my eyes. I see the hopes of God for humanity going up in flames. These flames represent real lives burning up because of the way we live.

The magnificent Temple built from exact plans God gave to David and Solomon stood resplendent. In the same way, God made plans for our individual lives that when fulfilled glorify Him. Time and time again we manage to mess up. He forgives us and helps us rebuild. In the same way, the Temple endured total destruction twice and numerous desecrations. Each time, God promised restoration. In 70AD, Titus destroyed the extraordinary Temple that Herod built. This story represents the Jewish people, and all they have suffered throughout the generations.

Sitting under the stars, watching the history of the Old City captivates us. Forty-five magical minutes fly by. The music stops and the walls go dark. Silently, our thoughts still enchanted, we follow the dispersing crowd. David and I are among the last exiting. We move slowly after a day of shopping and roaming the Old City streets. I pass a little lady standing by the door. I think she works here. I nod, say, "Thank you," smile, and walk on by. Our friend stops to talk with her. We wait while they talk. Soon our friend joins us. She gushes, "That's Marilyn Hickey. She doesn't know me from anybody. She just told me they are going to Gaza tomorrow." Simultaneously we ask out loud, "Why would anyone want to go to Gaza?" Well, I guess we know ministry can take you anywhere. More power to Marilyn Hickey!

THE EIGHTEENTH DAY

BUS 99

"When I came to you, brothers, I did not come with eloquence or superior wisdom as I proclaimed to you the testimony about God. For I resolved to know nothing while I was with you except Jesus Christ and him crucified. I came to you in weakness and fear, and with much trembling. My message and my preaching were not with wise and persuasive words, but with a demonstration of the Spirit's power, so that your faith might not rest on men's wisdom, but on God's power" (I Corinthians 2:1-5).

Sunday morning in Jerusalem offers a myriad of worship choices. David votes for attending Murad's church. Several people we met recently go there. The list starts with Zak (the coin dealer), then Johnny (Murad's brother), and others. All of them work in the Christian Quarter shops. We find them particularly outgoing and honest. Their pastor, Reverend Jack Y. Sara, must preach powerful messages. Getting to the Jerusalem Alliance Church involves meandering down a narrow cobblestone street for about half a mile.

A small sign over a single door along a long stone wall quietly identifies our destination. In Jerusalem, you never know what lies behind one of these unassuming doors. I expect a dark room. Instead, I find a brightly lit polished stone room with a gleaming staircase leading us upstairs to a simple, but light, clean sanctuary. Except for the altar in the front and the Arabic letters spelling "Jerusalem Alliance Church" across the top, it looks like any meeting room. A pleasant man comes up to us extending headphones, "English?" he asks. How do they always know?

Beautiful praise songs in Arabic start the service. Even with the different language, I feel comfortable and at home in this Arabic Christian Church. The young man leading the music energizes the congregation. He sings and dances like a man on fire for the Lord! Singers seated in the front rows of the congregation use microphones to back up the leader. This blessed praise time keeps going for over an hour. The pastor gets involved in the music. He accompanies the singers on the keyboard. Our earphones commence giving us hints as to song lyrics now and then. It takes several minutes for me to figure out who interprets. I spot a gray-haired lady wearing a pink dress sitting on the level above us. She speaks softly into a mike. Her young voice sounds like interpreters I heard on TV as a teenager watching UN proceedings. You know, back when Khrushchev angrily pounded his shoe on the table. The interpreter translated his excited words in even monotones, totally unemotional. Just interpret the facts, O.K. We don't see anyone we know from the Christian Quarter shops until Johnny comes in late and sits by a woman, presumably his wife. He looks surprised to see us.

A large group of men from the Philippines visit today. Other English speaking people also attend. I recognize one fellow as a guest at the Gloria. Now I wish I had spoken to him. Many days he sat alone at a table during breakfast engrossed in his computer. Lately, though, he meets with what look like professional men, perhaps teachers. The singing gets emotional. As the music crescendos, a man comes forward. He begins waving a big red flag to the music. A lot of the congregation gets involved. From time to time between songs, someone stands up reading Scripture aloud and comments on it. Most of the time they speak Arabic, sometimes English. It reminds me of Paul's instruction to the Corinthians regarding worship. *"What then shall we say, brothers? When you come together, everyone has a hymn, or a word of instruction, a revelation, a tongue or an interpretation. All of these must be done for the strengthening of the church"* (1 Corinthians 14:26).

The pastor gives up his keyboard to present the sermon. He welcomes the group from the Philippines. He shares that he received his Master's degree from their university. He preaches in Arabic. We get some of the message from the interpreter, but our headphones cut out often. The sermon encourages us to live holy lives in service to the Lord. Johnny stops and talks with us for a few minutes after the service. He and his wife teach children's Sunday school. He tells us he didn't have the benefit of being raised in a Christian home. Therefore, Johnny and his wife diligently make sure their children become grounded in the faith.

As an American Christian, I doubt seriously I have a clue as to what that means in Israel. In America, being raised in a Christian home creates positive influences in your life. You learn what it means to be a family under the care of a God who loves you and has a plan for your life. Parents pray together. They teach you how to pray. You go to church and learn to love your church family. People around you care about you. When burdened, you can go to them. They will help you. Bible study helps you know God's will for you. The Bible reveals gifts God gives you. You know you possess the fruit of the Spirit: love, joy, peace, patience, kindness, goodness, gentleness, faithfulness, and self-control. These gifts become part of you. You learn how to tap into them. You learn to control such things as anger and bitterness. Prayer becomes a significant part of life. You see God working all around you all of the time. Even non-Christians see you as holy rather than as a deceived cult.

Growing up a Christian in Israel must create all kinds of problems. You get all the same spiritual benefits as in America or anywhere else. Perhaps you receive even more spiritual blessing by living in the holy land. However, the pressures in Israel go beyond my imagination. Christianity makes up about 1% of the total Israeli population. Being such a minority means everyday life takes a toll. Israeli law prohibits anyone from evangelizing Jews. Imagine knowing the truth and being unable to share it with your neighbors.

On the other side, a child growing up with secular parents may never know God wants to bless him or her with His very presence. When confused about things like marriage, love, and the purpose of life, they become vulnerable to the false teachings of the world. For example, the world teaches anger needs to be expressed. Jesus teaches us to control ourselves and show love to others. Johnny's children learn what Jesus teaches.

Johnny led his mother to the Lord. Praise the Lord! We continue our conversation and end up staying at the church for about two and a half hours. We leave the church and turn up the narrow cobblestone street, with Muslim prayers loudly filling the air from the loudspeakers over the city.

We hope to catch the Bus 99 Tour of greater Jerusalem at 2:00 p.m. We barely have time to get back to the Gloria, eat a quick snack, pack up, and hike over to the bus stop. We make it at 1:50 p.m. We wait an hour discovering we cooled our jets at the wrong bus stop (thank you, Tourist Information Center). The next bus leaves at 4:17 p.m. from the stop somewhere downhill and one street over. To kill some time, we hurry through the traffic on the busy street and head to the modern mall to find my new journal. A stationary store, a pharmacy, and two bookstores later we remain empty handed. I admit to being picky about my journals! We sit on some steps, resting in the shade for a moment. Across the mall I see Marilyn Hickey sitting at an outside table at the Rimon Restaurant with a young couple. She slips on her Jackie-O sunglasses. I guess they got back from Gaza early.

There isn't much to do here but people-watch. Getting bored with Marilyn-watching, we trudge over to the correct bus stop. Perched on a Jerusalem limestone wall next to the bus stop, we enjoy one and a half hours of waiting and people-watching. I see a guy get off bus 20 who looks exactly like Rick Steves. A bus filled with school children pulls up and they descend and line up like little ducks to follow their teacher up the stairs. Tour groups pour out of the Old City and board their special waiting buses. Some Christian groups return to the Old City from their excursions elsewhere today. A school group gets off one bus. I think they live in another city. One young man wears a mask on his face with a metal bowl on his head. His friends, all about 12 years old, keep bonking each other on the head with this "metal helmet." The school guard carrying the machine gun looks about 14 years old, maybe 15.

You see lots of guns in Israel, slung over backs of soldiers or stuck into belt holsters. Some very big guns make the women look smaller. During the long wait my mind wanders. How can their tiny hands shoot such a large pistol? Somehow, I know they have done it many times and it both comforts and saddens me. The triggers don't seem under very close control. I'm curious about the safety mechanism used. Some pistols cabled to the belt cannot stray far from the owner. Are the guns locked and loaded? Could a crazy person grab a soldier's gun and start shooting? I've been sitting in the sun too long. Surely their training addresses that possibility.

The bus finally pulls up 30 minutes late and we start on our tour. As we board and pay David looks around for seating. Today the bus has lots of empty places. I speak up with, "What? You don't ride on the bottom deck of a double-decker bus. Let's go upstairs!"

This bus looks just like the double-decker red bus I rode in London a couple of years ago. It rained that day. Today no clouds materialize. We climb the stairs to the top level. We choose seats in front near the tall windshield. I grab the second row back and David sits right behind me. We plug in our headphones, choosing English from the eight languages on the dial. The bus takes off, practically burning rubber. I grip the handrail in front of me. With the driver trying to make up over half an hour, it looks like we're in for a thrilling ride!

On the top deck of Bus 99.

Two young boys sitting in front of me clench the rail in front of them. Laughing, eyes sparkling, they love this roller coaster bus ride. Their Dad sits across the aisle. All three wear black kippas with silver trim. The boys' earpieces keep falling out of their ears. Every few minutes the Dad gets up, does a balancing act crossing the aisle, and puts their ear plugs back in. He does well, considering the speed at which we travel. His devotion and patience with these two young Down syndrome boys impresses me.

Being on the top level magnifies every move the bus makes. Speed bumps do not deter our driver. Sharp curves take my breath away. He weaves in and out of traffic like a Volkswagen Bug. It reminds me of Mr. Toad's Wild Ride at Disney World. In less than two hours, our double-decker bus roars past eighty-five significant historical points of interest in the city of peace, Jerusalem. The recorded information on our headphones can't keep up with the driver. We constantly turn to see the site that just whizzed, by while headphones spew old information. By then we reach a new site. This driver intends to make it home by dinnertime.

Generally, we see quite a lot. New apartment buildings in East and West Jerusalem make us wonder about where they get all the needed water, electric, and sewer infrastructure. The hills of Jerusalem, covered with nice new apartment buildings, confirm continuous construction since 1967. Construction cranes loom everywhere. These high quality new neighborhoods look nothing like the *settlements* I imagine when people discuss new Jewish or Arab settlements.

Safra Square, King David (Eldan), Hahan, Haas Promenade, Jerusalem Mall, Biblical Zoo, Hertzel Museum, the Shrine of the Book, and the Knesset all fly by. The view from Haas Promenade impresses us. We would love to go back with a picnic and spend a day there. We zoom past the Shrine of the Book and remember seeing the Dead Sea Scrolls there ten years ago. Now that we can read some Hebrew letters, I would love to see the big Isaiah scroll again. We see the Knesset long enough to identify it. We pass the Crown Plaza Hotel where we stayed in 1999. Although the Crown Plaza treated us well, we treasure our time at the Gloria.

At Yad Vashem,[40] the holocaust museum, we race down the lovely tree lined avenue, screech a donut in the parking lot, and roar back down the lane. We get a glimpse of Yehuda Market, the Supreme Court, HaDavid Square, Hadassah Hospital[41], Mount Scopus, Augusta Victoria, Lion's Gate, the City of David, and Dung Gate among others. Laughing and having a great time, we both enjoy the ride and the tour.

---

40 Yad Vashem translates to Holocaust Martyrs' and Heroes' Remembrance Authority. The museum was established in 1953 through the Yad Vashem laws passed by Israel's parliament (the Knesset). Yad Vashem represents a living memorial to the six million Jews who perished in the holocaust during World War II.
41 Hadassah Hospital was established in 1939, the first teaching hospital established in what was then known as Palestine. Hadassah, established in 1912 in New York City, was started for the purpose of providing health care in Ottoman-occupied Jerusalem. In 2005, Hadassah was nominated for the Nobel Peace Prize, in recognition of its efforts to provide services to all, irrespective of ethnic and religious differences, and its efforts to build peace.

The bus dumps us and we hike up the hill, freezing. The chill surprises us. We expected to be back earlier and forgot jackets. We decide to do a real American-type dinner and call Domino's for take out. A Domino's exists near the hotel, but the phones trick us. We settle for pop and chips.

THE NINETEENTH DAY

BIBLE LANDS MUSEUM

"The sons of Noah who came out of the ark were Shem, Ham and Japheth. (Ham was the father of Canaan.) These were the three sons of Noah, and from them came the people who were scattered over the earth" (Genesis 9:18-19).

Yesterday, we spent so much time observing the activity at the bus stop that we felt smart enough to try the public transportation system. We noticed bus 20 came by every five or ten minutes toward Ben Yehuda shopping center. Our search for my new journal exhausted local possibilities. Now we must expand our horizons. We board bus 20 to Ben Yehuda. This place resembles Pearl Street Mall in Boulder, Colorado, mid-east style. The construction for light rail complicates traffic and all other matters, western style! Ben Yehuda shopping mall offers welcome changes from the aggressive sellers at the souk. We find a book store and ask for journals, "You know, a book with blank pages?" No luck. Next we come upon an office supply store. They have something with papyrus pages, probably for sketching, but I like it. I get two of them and stickers to decorate the plain gray cardboard covers. These stickers make my journal unique with pictures of Jerusalem all over the front. These additional journals should last through the rest of our stay.

David mentions we should replace the camera I lost. Being in Jerusalem without a camera can only be described as pure torture. Photo Prisma stocks the very same camera I lost, even in pink! I must have pink to match my computer. Everything about the camera mirrors the old one except the Hebrew writing on the box and Hebrew instructions, which look like something from a museum because of the Hebrew. David adds a pink camera case for me, hoping to avoid another loss. Using my brand new camera, I take a picture of the salesman and David. I ask David to take a picture, using the new camera, of me with the salesman. Out of the shop on the street, I begin shooting pictures of everything. The light rail construction, the shop fronts, shops across the street, flowers, trees, people, people walking up the street, people walking down the street, signs, street signs, store signs – EVERYTHING! I want to bring Jerusalem home with me. If I can't take the city home, I endeavor taking as many pictures as possible with me. Having a camera again feels so good. Praise the Lord!

At Ben Yehuda Square, we stop for Kosher Lemonade. My face involuntarily winces. It tastes extremely tart! Thankfully, David brought a packet of sweetener. I recover and start people watching. The variety of people here intrigues me. Across the square a man plays his bright red guitar. Another man rushes by with a huge bouquet of flowers. Bedouins, Orthodox Jews, teenagers, moms and babies, all kind of people flock to the mall. We watch from a table in front of Shawarma Falafel. Armed guards carrying serious machine guns patrol the mall. Some differences exist between Pearl Street Mall back home and Ben Yehuda. The bloody history of Ben Yehuda can't be overlooked.

On September 4, 1997, three suicide bombs killed eight people, wounding nearly 200 other innocents in Ben Yehuda Mall. One fatality held dual United States/Israeli citizenship. Seven of the wounded claimed U. S. citizenship. On January 16, 2002, I first heard Benjamin Netanyahu call these suicide bombers *homicide bombers* at a speech he gave in Denver. Since then, I've heard the term often. I can't help but think about those who have violently died here at Ben Yehuda Shopping Mall and throughout Israel. Even so, I feel safe in Jerusalem.

Strolling down the street we find a shop selling only kippas. They have every kind of kippa imaginable. Every professional sports team in the United States gets representation. We find a Denver Broncos kippa, gray on white. I tell the merchant, "No, it's orange on blue." He points to the blue and orange one. It says, *Denver Nuggets!*

Nearby, a scarf and accessories store catches my eye. We find a hat for me and scarves for friends back home. Lunchtime finds us in front of familiar golden arches – McDonald's![42] The word kosher surprises us. A big Mac, some fries, cokes with ice, a brownie, and some ice cream later, we resume shopping. Sauntering down the mall we come upon an incredible bakery. Cookies, rolls and all kinds of baked goods look over the top, in

---

42 In Israel, all McDonald's restaurants serve kosher meat. However, not all of McDonald's restaurants are strictly kosher in Israel. Those restaurants that strictly observe Kashrut (kosher laws) are closed on Shabbat and all religious holidays, and do not mix meat and dairy products together. Big Macs are served without cheese.

more ways than one. Delicious goodies piled high on large trays make them irresistible. David enjoys a couple of pizza rolls. Sambooki's must be the most famous bakery in town.

Shopping and eating at Ben Yehuda makes for lots of fun, but we need to change activities. We grab a taxi to the Bible Lands Museum Jerusalem. In 1998-99, we visited the Shrine of the Book and the Israeli Museum. Both extraordinary museums we highly recommend. We hope the Bible Lands Museum Jerusalem impresses as much. On the way over I snap pictures from the back window of the taxi. Storefronts, soldiers, Orthodox Jewish men and women, school kids, police vehicles, flags, signs, motorcycles, people talking on cell phones, people on Segways,[43] and a man talking on a cell phone while driving a Segway. The driver humors us by passing by the walking bridge under construction called David's Harp. This dramatic work of art looks like a huge harp in the middle of the city. I shoot pictures of every angle as we drive away.

Before entering the Bible Lands Museum Jerusalem, I take David's picture under the sign. Then I'm forced to retire my precious camera to its pretty pink case. They don't allow picture taking in the museum.

43 A Segway is a two-wheeled electric vehicle operated while standing.

The Bible Land Museum Jerusalem *Guide to the Collection* introduces the founders and explains the history of this fantastic collection. Let's take a peek into the founding of this museum through their book.

The Bible Lands Museum Jerusalem represents the lifework and dedication of Batya and Elie Borowski, the founders of the museum who have worked together to design, build and establish the only museum in the world dedicated to the history of the biblical period.

Dr. Elie Borowski, renowned scholar and collector of ancient art, carefully accumulated the objects in the museum over more than half a century. Beginning with his first acquisition in 1943, of a cylinder seal engraved in ancient Hebrew (Aramaic) letters with the name "Shallum", he began to build one of the world's most important collections of ancient Near Eastern artifacts with the specific aim of placing the Bible in its historical context.

Born in Warsaw in 1913, Dr. Borowski studied at the Mir Yeshiva and went on to study for the rabbinate at the Collegio Rabbinico Italiano in Florence. At that time he became enamoured of the art and history of the ancient Near East and decided to devote his life to studying it.

At the Pontifical Biblical Institute in Rome he learned to read cuneiform and specialized in early Sumerian writings.

Just before the outbreak of the Second World War, in August 1939, while studying at the Sorbonne in Paris, Elie Borowski enlisted with a unit of Jewish volunteers of the French army to fight the Nazis. As a military internee in Switzerland, he worked part time for the Museum of Art and History of Geneva, studying their collection of Mesopotamian seals and cuneiform tablets.

Devastated by the loss of his family during the Holocaust, Elie Borowski felt there was no point in art and music, poetry and literature if they could not provide people with the moral courage to withstand injustice and barbarism. The need for an awakening of moral and spiritual values contained in the Bible, gradually developed

138

into a lifetime goal. He believed the most effective way to reach this goal was to assemble a collection of artifacts from the lands of the Bible that would confirm and elucidate the riches of the biblical world with its ethics and spirituality.

Over the years, Elie Borowski put together a choice collection of objects. Each seal, relief or figurine documents some event or person, or interprets some story or custom of our ancient past. Together these artifacts make up a mosaic of the ancient world, painting as rich a picture as possible of the daily lives, religious rituals and historic events that we know about through the Bible and through biblical archaeology.

Elie and Batya Borowski are a brilliant combination of the scholarly and the practical. Batya Borowski, formerly of New York, combined her business acumen with Elie Borowski's scholarship and set the wheels in motion for the building of this museum. With intense dedication and tireless effort, they unrelentingly pursued the realization of their dream.

In 1985 the groundbreaking ceremony was held on the site where the museum stands today. On May 11, 1992 the Bible Lands Museum Jerusalem opened for Israel and the world.[44]

One can only imagine what transpired during those seven years between the ground breaking and the opening ceremony. The collection itself rates ultra-exceptional. These artifacts rival treasures I inspected in the British Museum two years ago. Unlike the British Museum, here Scripture accompanies every exhibit. Refreshingly, each display increases the viewer's faith by showing Bible verses in the historical context. For instance, the very first exhibit, called the family of man, references Genesis 10:32, *"These are the families of the sons of Noah, after their generations, in their nations; and of these were the nations divided in the earth after the flood."* The exhibit shows a map of the descendants of Shem, Ham, and Japheth. The artifacts show differences and similarities between the descendants of Noah's sons. We take our time going from section to section. Around 4:30 we arrive at

---

44 Taken from *Bible Lands Museum Guide of the Collection*, Jerusalem, 2002. Used by permission.

Room 20 and look for the obligatory gift shop exit. A few purchases later our taxi arrives. I take pictures all the way to Jaffa Gate.

Recovery comes quickly. Eager to get out again, we opt for a trip to the Church of the Holy Sepulcher this evening. By early evening, tour groups return to their hotels outside the Old City for dinner. We expect a quiet time of prayer and reflection. The Church of the Holy Sepulcher stands over Golgotha, the place of the Crucifixion and the tomb of Jesus. The crucifixion took place outside the city walls. However, the city walls changed since that momentous day and now include the holy site of the Church of the Holy Sepulcher. Divine intervention preserved this place. Not all intervention seems good at the time, but in this case it helped identify the place of Jesus' crucifixion.

The Roman Emperor, Hadrian, wanted to root out every remembrance of the Jewish and Christian religions. He destroyed Calvary and the Tomb of Jesus, and built a temple on it to worship the Roman god, Jupiter. God uses everything. Hadrian thought he could eradicate the site from the face of the earth. However, his temple to Jupiter actually marked the site as the place where Jesus died and resurrected. Helena, mother of the Roman Emperor Constantine the Great, upon her conversion to Christianity, traveled to the Holy Land. Her quest identified the site of the crucifixion. In 326AD, Constantine demolished Hadrian's temple and built a majestic Christian church. The Persians destroyed it in 614AD. Because of its significance, Abbot Modestos rebuilt the church on a smaller scale, only to be destroyed in 1009 by the Khalif Hakem.

The Crusaders built the present church. God used persecution, greed, and even violence to preserve this site. As much as we like Gordon's Golgotha and the Garden Tomb, the archaeological evidence points to this as the historical site of Jesus' death. It has been preserved throughout history. But, in spite of all the evidence, many remain unconvinced. Protestants often label it a traditional site, instead of an historical site. Ten years ago David had no desire to enter the Church of the Holy Sepulcher. His prejudices forced his eyes to focus on physical things like candles and icons. Tonight, his eyes of faith hunger to see as much as his heart desires to bow at this precious place.

Only a few minutes stroll through the Christian Quarter positions us in the small square in front of the church. Cool, crisp air reminds us of evening. More people than we expect stand in the square and around the huge arched front doors. We observe an exhausted tour group gathering to leave. I begin taking numerous pictures of the square, the massive front door, the arched windows above, and the famous ladder under one of those second story windows. The ladder serves as a marvelous example of how having six different religious sects governing the Church of the Holy Sepulcher continues the struggle that plagued it throughout centuries. Since 1857, this out of place ladder overlooks the square. Arguments over who the ladder belonged to and who has the right to remove it continued for decades. The people managing the Church at the time decided to leave it there. So the famous ladder sits above the beautiful entrance to the Church. Even more interesting is the fact that the ladder I now focus for a picture is not the original ladder! The original wooden ladder deteriorated and had to be replaced. I wonder how they decided who had the right to do that! Perhaps the groups cooperate better these days.

The stone of Unction sits just inside the front entrance. Unction means anointing. This smooth, polished red and black stone about 10 feet long and 3 feet wide marks the place Jesus' body laid while being washed and prepared for burial. This stone has been memorialized since medieval times. The present stone dates from 1810. Many historical sites look like traditional sites these days because of the vast amount of decoration and ornamentation within them. In my own experience, the traditional site versus historical site discussion often distracts from the holiness of the site. This place commands respect and reverence for my Lord and Savior.

On the main floor, we pass by huge granite columns, down corridors lined with works of art from the greats. Arches tower over us as we make our way to the tomb. We wait in a short line while people crawl into the tomb where Jesus laid. Here people pray on the marble slab covering the rock on which Christ's body laid. The short line moves slowly as some linger to pour hearts out to God. Our turn barely starts when a man abruptly sticks his head in the cave and commences yelling, "Quickly, quickly, now." He has the audacity to start clapping his hands, "quickly, quickly." No one can pray with the racket he makes. I ask the Lord to forgive him as we get off our knees and stoop over to leave through the small opening. We back out of the cave in respectful fashion to find this rude man leading a tour! His tour runs behind schedule. The obviously secular guide pushes to get the group through this tomb and on to their waiting dinner. I feel especially bad for the young woman praying in the very corner. At one point she quietly murmurs, "One moment."

He yells back, "Quickly, quickly." What a jerk! Who knows how far she traveled and what she sacrificed to be here, kneeling at the tomb of her Savior. David fumes. I told him I asked the Lord to forgive the rude man. With a scowl on his face David growls, "Well I haven't forgiven him." David came here to pray. This man made it impossible.

Up tall steep stone stairs we climb to the Greek Orthodox Chapel. An altar stands over the rocky outcrop on which Christ's cross stood. We view the Rock of Golgotha through protective glass. A hole underneath the altar enables one to actually touch the stone. David goes first. The Greek Orthodox Priest reminds tourists, "No pictures, no pictures." The camera toting tourists fade back for a few minutes. When they think the priest leaves they reappear. Again, he chases them away. This happens half a dozen times while David prays under the altar, on his knees at the foot of the cross. He prays in peace here. He experiences an awesome encounter with God. No one waits to pray here at this time so he continues praying for several minutes. David recognizes the goodness of God. God gave him an even better prayer spot with this authoritative priest keeping people from distracting him. Now he asks God to forgive the rude guide. David prays the guide can find joy and peace in Christ. With tears in his eyes he comes back to sit with me. I respectfully approach the altar. As I get on my knees to crawl underneath the altar, I fail to notice the Priest opening his Bible to start the Greek Orthodox evening service. I continue my prayer begun at the tomb before being interrupted.

Lord, I started this prayer in the tomb. It was the right prayer in the wrong place. I was praying and thanking You for Your suffering, but the tomb is where You resurrected. This is the place where You suffered for us, for me. This is the place You, the Perfect Sacrifice, took on the sin of the world. You did this so we could be free from sin and death and so that we could have relationship with You. You were beaten beyond recognition before they brought You here and nailed You to a cross.

Suddenly, the enormity of what He did for me here, at this very place on the cross, strikes me with heavy force. Tears begin to flow. I slowly reach my hand down into the black hole, stretching my fingertips until I touch the cold stone. Overcome with emotion, I back out from under the altar and go sit next to David, sobbing and praying.

The Church of the Holy Sepulcher remains remarkable because, in spite of the many tourists that come here, you can still pray and worship. The reverent, quiet atmosphere leads to introspection. Free admission encourages pilgrims to come and pray here. No rules bar Protestants or anyone else. Depending on the person and the situation, the experience here could be more devout than at the Temple in Jesus' day. Remember, Jesus threw money changers out of the Temple. Guards kept Gentile converts in the outer courts away from the Temple.

We finish our day by approaching the Western Wall. As I stand here praying I think about all we saw and did today. I remember a book I once read by Randall Price called *The Stones Cry Out.* I felt the stones cry out on this night. I felt the Unction Stone cry out at the death of Jesus and the natural, unfailing feelings of emptiness and loss combined with the disciples' uncertainty for the future. I felt the Rock of Golgotha cry out for the anguish, pain, and suffering as it witnessed the perfect sacrifice. I felt the stone on which Christ's body laid in the tomb as a final resting place. I felt that stone cry out, "Victory," when He rose again. And finally, tonight, when I press my fingertips against this stone Wall, I feel centuries of prayers reverberating, crying out, for His return. Yes, Mr. Price, the stones do cry out. Tonight as I touch them their cries fill my heart.

THE TWENTIETH DAY

DOME OF THE ROCK

"But the king replied to Araunah, 'No, I insist on paying you for it. I will not sacrifice to the Lord my God burnt offerings that cost me nothing.' So David bought the threshing floor and the oxen and paid fifty shekels of silver for them. David built an altar to the Lord there and sacrificed burnt offerings and fellowship offerings" (II Samuel 24:24-25).

We need to get moving while it's still early because of the hot day. I can hardly believe we have less than a week left of our Jerusalem adventure. We schedule a visit to the Dome of the Rock today. As a teenager, I remember reading a book with a picture of the inside of the Shrine of the Dome of the Rock. I had no idea the significance of the Rock with the big gold dome over it. I never suspected I would ever get near it. In 1998, I saw the inside of the Dome of the Rock. Now tourists cannot go into the buildings. We can go onto the Temple Mount before or after Muslim prayers. A Muslim man selling frozen bottles of water charges us only $1 each. Every other place charges $2 for water not frozen. We feel blessed. Frozen water on this hot day makes sense. Then the man begins to tell us why we cannot go into the Dome of the Rock and Jews cannot come on the Temple Mount.

"In 2000 Ariel Sharon came up here and attacked our men while they were sock footed, on their prayer mats. Over fifty people died that day. Jews want to kick us off this place. They think their Temple was once here, but they can't prove it." I want to correct him. Reminding myself that I'm his guest, I keep my mouth shut and move on. Revisionist history fuels hatred.

The online Jewish Virtual Library features the story behind the story most Americans miss. *The al-Aksa Intifada,* an article by Mitchell Bard, reports:

Ariel Sharon visited the Temple Mount on September 28, 2000 after receiving clearance for his visit from Palestinian security chief

Jabril Rejoub. Rejoub assured Sharon if he did not enter the mosques there would be no problem. Sharon did not enter, or attempt to enter any mosques. He remained there 34 minutes during normal visiting hours open to tourists. Around 1,500 Palestinian youths shouted slogans trying to stir up trouble. The presence of 1,500 hundred Israeli police forestalled impending violence. After Sharon left the Temple Mount, outbreaks of stone throwing continued, injuring 28 Israeli policemen. No official reports of Palestinian deaths or injuries happened that day. The situation escalated over the next days and weeks with Palestinians' own radio stations misinforming them. Palestinian mobs used this incident to attack shrines and destroy Joseph's tomb in Nablus. They stoned worshipers at the Western Wall and attacked Rachel's Tomb in Bethlehem. Arafat engineered this uprising, referred to as the al-Aksa intifada. Palestinian Authority Communications Minister, Imad Faluji, later admitted Arafat planned the uprising back in July as Arafat's response to the United States' conditions for peace in the Middle East, long before Sharon's visit to the Temple Mount.[45]

We walk past al-Aksa with its brown shoe bins lined up outside the doors. We turn left facing the golden dome. Built in 691AD, the Dome of the Rock occupies the Temple Mount. In 1998, while standing on the Kotel plaza, our professor, Wink Thompson, told us to look toward the path going up the hill next to the Western Wall. If the huge green door at the top stood open, we could visit the Temple Mount and perhaps venture into the mosques.

I remember one rainy day another student and I were at the Wall when we noticed the open green door. We got excited and scurried up the hill through security onto Temple Mount. The chilly day made any shelter look good. We turned at the first right, quickly took off our shoes and deposited them in the brown shoe bins. Shivering, we rushed into what we thought was the Dome of the Rock. I remember consulting my guide book, *The Holy Land* by Jerome Murphy-O'Connor, as we inspected the inside. I said to my friend suspiciously, "This place doesn't have marble floors and mosaics like this book describes." I kept looking around. The columns in this mosque definitely differed from the guide book's description. In his

---

45 Taken by permission, Jewish Virtual Library, 'The Palestinian War,' (September 2000-2005) 'The al-Aksa Intifada' by Mitchell Bard. www.JewishVirtualLibrary.org

book, Murphy O'Connor mentions the garden like mosaics of the interior. I saw no mosaics. I saw no crosses on columns mentioned in the book. We were not in the Dome of the Rock! As we turned to walk out of the al-Aksa Mosque, the doorway framed the huge gold dome at the other end of the Temple Mount. Boy, did I feel foolish. I don't remember about my friend, but my face was red.

David — the Dome of the Rock is behind you!

Inside the Dome of the Rock along the top of the inner octagon we noticed the beautiful Arabic writing. Later I discovered the translation actually warns Christians to relinquish their faith in Jesus as the Messiah. I'm sure many Christian tourists saw it and only thought of it as a beautiful expression of writing in a different and strange language. Instead it warns Christians to deny the Trinity – or else!

The Temple Mount covers over 35 acres. The Golden Dome of the Rock, Al-Aksa Mosque, the dome of the prophet, dome of the chain, a school, a women's mosque, the dome of learning (grammar college), and a couple of huge absolution fountains all reside on Temple Mount. Remembering what we learned on our *dig* regarding the illegal extension of Temple Mount by the Muslims, David strolls over to inspect the area for himself. Solomon's Stables, the ancient arches helping support the Temple Mount, show new construction. Two emergency exits display tall retractable doors.

David remarks that the Solomon Stables bulldozer fiasco cost archaeologists a precious chance to research artifacts in situ on Temple Mount. In a way the Muslims have a point, too. They needed more room for Muslims to pray during Ramadan. Archaeologists would have taken 25 – 50 years to clear the area before allowing any building to occur. Could any government fairly balance the archaeologists' desires with the Muslim's objectives?

The area next to the Golden Gate is off limits to tourists. Non-Muslims may not set their unholy feet in this holy area. David observes a kick ball game by a bunch of rowdy teens having fun, instead of the reverent site he expects. In general, Temple Mount quietly invites reflection and prayers. Unfortunately, the authorities do not allow Christians or Jews to pray here.

The brochure tells us we must leave before morning prayers. When these prayers dismiss, it becomes a mass of humanity, too crowded for me. At 10:15 we head to our green door. Soldiers direct us to a different green door, across the way and downstairs, marking our exit. That door dumps us in the Muslim Quarter, on our way to the Western Wall. The noise and graffiti on Chain Street sharply contrasts with the manicured and quiet Temple Mount.

Once again we find ourselves at the Wall. Walking toward the woman's side I recall my encounter with the Lord yesterday. Lots of women pray here today. Even so, it isn't difficult to get a place next to the Wall. My time prayer simply consists of a time of praise and gratitude to Him Who makes all things possible. I pray ten minutes and begin my slow walk backward. You don't turn your back on God or on the Wall! We meet at the plaza and turn toward the City of David, below us. As we leave, it occurs to me that no one ever argues with guards here. Guards have guns, big ones. A memorial just outside the security gates at Dung Gate honors Shlomo Goren, "in memory of Major General Shlomo Goren First Chief Rabbi of Israeli Defense Forces and Chief Rabbi of Israel. President of the Supreme Rabbinical Court of Israel. Outstanding Torah Scholar and Great Halachic Authority. Leader of the Liberators of the Temple Mount and the Western Wall." A lot of memorials exist in Israel.

The road from Dung Gate to the City of David slopes downhill. Steep and difficult to navigate paths force me to use my cane. The City of David slogan proclaims, "Where it all started." Well, so far it all started on Mount Moriah with Adam. It all started in Jericho where Joshua crossed the Jordan. It all started in Hebron, from where David first ruled. History confirms David and Solomon's rule from Jerusalem as Israel's Golden Age. The City of David located south of Temple Mount, stands surrounded by the Kidron Valley on the east, the Tyropeon Valley on the west, and the Hinnom Valley the south. Perched above its source of water, the Gihon Spring nourished the City of David. It flows to this day. These few blocks lie vulnerably exposed on the side of the hill. Archaeological ruins of monumental walls, tall towers, along with an advanced water system, testify Salem (previous name for Jerusalem) at one time stood invincible. The first sign of this being a fortified city goes back to the time of Abraham (see Genesis 14:17-20).

Centuries later, King David made Salem his capitol. Our first stop, area G, includes stepped stone structures from the Jebusite period. Archaeologists found several First Temple period dwellings belonging to the rich and famous. The House of Ahiel had an indoor toilet and furniture made out of imported wood. A big find lay hidden at the bottom of the excavation pit. The scribes of old often protected their documents with special clay seals called bullae. Jeremiah's scribe, Burach, signed some of the over 50 bullae uncovered in area G.

> *"From the room of Gemariah son of Shaphan the secretary, which was in the upper courtyard at the entrance of the New Gate of the temple, Baruch read to all the people at the Lord's temple the words of Jeremiah from the scroll" (Jeremiah 36:10).*

Area G includes a burned out room containing numerous arrowheads indicating destruction by the Babylonians. This small area confirms an incredible amount of Biblical history.

The water system fascinates archaeologists. The Gihon Spring surfaces in the lower part of the eastern slope of the city. Sometime during the Middle Bronze Period, residents dug a secret underground tunnel leading to a secured pool to protect their precious water supply. Charles Warren explored this tunnel in 1867. Many people believe David used Warren's shaft to conquer the city.

> *"The king and his men marched to Jerusalem to attack the Jebusites, who lived there. The Jebusites said to David, 'You will not get in here; even the blind and the lame can ward you off.' They thought, 'David cannot get in here.' Nevertheless, David captured the fortress of Zion, the City of David.*
>
> *On that day, David said, "Anyone who conquers the Jebusites will have to use the water shaft to reach those 'lame and blind' who are David's enemies." That is why they say, "The ' lame and blind' will not enter the palace."*
>
> *David then took up residence in the fortress and called it the City of David. He built up the area around it, from the supporting terraces inward. And he became more and more powerful, because the Lord God Almighty was with him" (II Samuel 5:6-10).*

In order to view Warren's Shaft, we traverse a series of spiral staircases. The sight of the shaft itself surprises me. It's barely large enough for one man to crawl through. I try to imagine the bravery of Joab, who silently climbed that shaft in the dark to win the city for his King. From the top of the shaft we continue down more stairs to the split in the tunnel. Here you must choose whether to go through Hezekiah's tunnel or the Canaanite Tunnel. Hezekiah's tunnel involves a three-foot deep, constant flow of cold water, from the Gihon Spring. Flashback to 1998. Craig and I slogged through that water with the rest of our class (dubbed the 'dirty dozen' because there were twelve of us). The narrow dark tunnel demands flashlights. Claustrophobia makes me vie for last place in the tribal line. One young man with a more serious case won. He walked in back, then me, then Craig and the rest of the group ahead. The ceiling varied from low to very high. Without the flashlight, I could not see my hand in front of my face.

The cold water level raised and lowered on my body because of uneven ground. Someone ahead occasionally called out, "Step!" We slowed down until getting past the rock or hole in the ground under water. One of the women in the group started singing, *"Spring Up O Well."* Hearing all the voices chime in calmed my claustrophobic fears. Five hundred ninety yards later, the sight of natural light allowed me to release my grip on Craig's shoulder.

David and I choose the Canaanite tunnel. At one hundred twenty five yards long, this tunnel provided irrigation before Hezekiah dug his famous tunnel. The narrow foot path prevents me from standing with my feet side by side. I turn sideways in order to get through. The dim lighting provides comfort. Thankful for the light, I remember Hezekiah's tunnel forces you to use your own flashlight to light the path. I get a little claustrophobic. All the other tourists chose to slog through Hezekiah's tunnel. Once again, we choose the road less traveled. The smooth floor of this tunnel proves water flowed through here to a reservoir in the southern part of the city. David's knee forces him to move slowly and choose his steps carefully in the uneven footing. Anticipating freedom, I sprint ahead.

Walking the Canaanite Tunnel.

Getting out in the warm sun feels good. The tunnels remain cool all year. We hike down another steep hill to catch the van back to the City of David entry gate. Our shuttle has a knee high step up to get in. I hesitate, trying to figure out what to grab onto. With effort I make it. I sure don't want to trudge back up that hill.

Next we go see the movie exhibit! I love movie exhibits. This one meets in a tiny cooled theater. We get a 15 minute 3D history about the

City of David. Afterward, we decide to taxi back to Jaffa Gate. A huge van pulls up and says, "taxi?" We are only two people. The van looks like it seats at least 14. We ignore the guy. He flips a U-turn and pulls up beside us. "You want taxi?"

David says, "We're only going to Jaffa Gate."

"O.K.," he pulls the van door open. Again, I am faced with a knee high step. I have difficulty. The driver encourages me by saying, "You can do it, Madam. You're still young!" I have to laugh. I don't feel very young at the moment. After all the hills and steps I have been on today, I feel like I am 100!

It turns out we get the ride in the huge van because the driver dropped off his tour. He has an hour or so before he has to pick them up. Being an enterprising young man, he takes advantage of his situation. He drops us at Jaffa Gate. David mentions seeing a hamburger sign on a nearby restaurant. A hamburger, fries, coke; life is good. It doesn't taste quite like a hamburger at home. It's close enough and the fries are right on. Afterward, I feel the bathroom call from Pharaoh's Fury. I leave David to settle the bill while I scoot up the hill to the Gloria. I make it without embarrassing myself. I feel much better now. We relax, looking forward to tomorrow.

THE TWENTY-FIRST DAY

THE SECRET GARDEN

"It is a land the Lord your God cares for; the eyes of the Lord your God are continually on it from the beginning of the year to its end" (Deuteronomy 11:12).

Today we tour Bridges for Peace. At 9:30 a.m., the taxi drivers at Jaffa Gate have a confab about the address. Finally, one of them saunters over. He says, "You come with me. I know where it is." O.K., but I can't tell what he knows from the discussion and confused looks. Surprisingly, he drives right to it. The street resembles an alley. The gated compound opens only after the taxi driver begs to turn his large taxi around in their parking lot. Our friend, Charleeda, works here. She leads us into a lovely courtyard with neatly trimmed grass, decorated with splashes of floral color along the sides of a winding path. Around to the entrance we approach a manicured front patio. Up the stairs and inside the office, security screens report parking lot activity to the receptionist. Bridges for Peace rents the property from the Ethiopian Church next door. They built the magnificent main building around the turn of the 20th century for the Queen of Ethiopia. She never came to Jerusalem. Bridges occupies two buildings on the compound plus some apartments for workers and volunteers just outside the gate.

Upstairs, Charleeda shows us her tiny cubicle. She introduces her volunteer assistant, a woman here for three months from Arizona. Charleeda and this woman take care of the administration and proofreading part of Publications. At one time, Bridges for Peace had four graphic artists, but only two remain because of changes in visa laws.

Marnus Schoeman steals us away to show us how Bridges for Peace attempts to heal divisions between Christians and Jews. Marnus hails from a small town about 50 miles south of Johannesburg, South Africa. Before visiting the food bank and distribution center, Marnus explains Bridges for Peace. The mission statement declares, "Bridges for Peace is a Jerusalem-based, Bible believing Christian organization supporting Israel and building relationships between Christians and Jews worldwide through education and practical deeds expressing God's love and mercy." Here, Christians serve Jews in love without trying to evangelize them. By serving Jews without trying to change them, volunteers show unconditional love. Bridges for Peace outreach includes, but is not limited to, eleven areas described in their brochure.

1. Adoption – sponsors can adopt an Israeli individual or family for one year, providing food, bus tickets, and financial assistance for special needs and becoming personally connected by exchanging letters.

2. Feed a Child – provides hot school lunches, birthday and holiday gifts, school books, a backpack filled with supplies, and funds for special needs during the summer.

3. Welcome Program – new immigrants get a large gift package that includes a kitchen set of pans and utensils, blankets, school kits for the children, and a 3-volume Hebrew-Russian (or 2-volume Hebrew-Spanish) edition of the Hebrew Scriptures.

4. Home Repair – teams of skilled construction workers renovate homes of the poor and elderly in dire conditions, fixing leaky plumbing, plastering, rewiring, and installing cabinets.

5. Project Rescue – pays for passports, visas, ground transportation, and lodging for Jewish people in the countries of the Diaspora who want to immigrate to Israel.

6. Cheer baskets – filled with cookies, candies, nuts and tea – bringing hope and encouragement to victims of terrorism, shut-ins, and the elderly who need a tangible expression of God's love.

7. Dental – for people who suffer from tooth pain.

8. Food – distribution of food to needy Israeli families, also assists Jewish organizations serving the poor.

9. Adopt an Israeli town – currently Bridges for Peace assists 15 Israeli towns from the Galilee to the Negev that are experiencing severe economic hardship. They work with community officials, giving out parcels of food for needy families.

10. Project TIKVA (Hope) – soup kitchens provide hot, nutritious meals – often the only meal eaten in a day – for elderly and sick Jewish people

who cannot emigrate [sic] to Israel. Heaters are purchased for the winter season for those living in unheated quarters.

11. Victims of war – they minister to anyone touched by terrorism, delivering special cheer baskets to the wounded in hospitals after a suicide bombing and to the bereaved. Special needs, such as wheelchairs, food vouchers, and financial assistance for medical bills are provided for those in long-term rehabilitation.[46]

Bridges for Peace often writes – Don't just read Bible prophecy – be part of it! Their good work inspires me.

Henry Blackaby teaches, "Find out where God is at work and join Him." Bridges for Peace volunteers pay their own travel expenses to Israel to help God restore thousands of families to Eretz Yisrael (the Land). God continues drawing His people back to the Land. Throughout Scripture, He tells us he will draw them from north, south, east, and west.

> *"Do not be afraid, for I am with you; I will bring your children from the east and gather you from the west. I will say to the north, 'Give them up!' and to the south, 'Do not hold them back.' Bring my sons from afar and my daughters from the ends of the earth – everyone who is called by my name, whom I created for my glory, whom I formed and made" (Isaiah 43:5-7).*

The educational arm of Bridges for Peace enlightens Christians regarding our Jewish roots. Outside the teaching room, a board with stones embedded in it grabs David's attention. Marnus explains the unusual antique. After cutting wheat or barley with a scythe, the stalks would be thrown on the threshing floor and an animal would pull the heavy board with the embedded stones over the stalks. This separates the wheat out of the heads so it could be winnowed in the wind. The beaters in a modern combine do the same thing. There are many references in the Bible about separating the wheat from the chaff. *"Not so the wicked! They are like chaff that the wind blows away"* (Psalm 1:4). *"I will scatter you like chaff driven by the desert wind"* (Jeremiah 13:24).

Kathryn, a volunteer from Australia, shows us the teaching room while Marnus loads the van with items needing delivery as we travel across

46 Taken from Bridges for Peace Brochure, Jerusalem, Israel, by permission

town. Entering the teaching room transports us back to the time of Christ. Flickering wall lamps evoke the feeling of candlelight. A wooden ladder with rope tied rungs leans against one stucco wall. The walls themselves have bits of straw artfully embedded into the stucco. We sit on a couch with pillows drinking all of it in. Last night they held a Passover Seder and taught a tour group about deliverance. Some tour groups have each person bring a suitcase full of items like toothbrushes and toiletries to donate to Bridges for distribution to needy families. Bridges likes to thank them with a special teaching in this room. Last night, the group ate authentic kosher food prepared by a small Jewish restaurant across town. Today, Marnus gives us a quick lesson in Jewish relations. He must return the pots unwashed because washing the pots in an un-kosher way would make them non-kosher and useless to the family restaurant.

We jump into the loaded van and race across town to the Jerusalem food bank. The food bank distribution center parking lot lies behind locked gates requiring a cell phone call to gain entrance. The gate locks behind us. As we exit our vehicle, I notice Marnus locks the doors. The food bank recently quadrupled in size since its beginnings in 1990. This indicates how much people want to help. In spite of this global recession, Bridges for Peace's giving, as of April 2009, is up 14%. God is amazing! Bridges for Peace helps the Israeli economy by buying food locally and distributing the food to the needy. This creates a double blessing for the Land. We meet the receptionist and two women packing pallets with food and supplies for delivery. All ages of people volunteer here. We stay for another half hour while Marnus describes how they distribute food and supplies in Jerusalem and other towns throughout Israel.

With lunchtime upon us, we ask Marnus to drop us off at the famous restaurant Ticho House. A restaurant of local legend it includes one of the city's loveliest examples of an Arab mansion. Dr. Abraham Ticho, a famous Jewish ophthalmologist, used to give the poor free treatment, irrespective of their ethnic origin or religion. His artist wife, Anna, kept a busy social life. By day a clinic, by night their home became the center of Jerusalem's social and intellectual life. Now it's a restaurant with a museum administered by the Israel Museum.

We meet a couple of friends here who highly recommend it. They rave about the food. The restaurant overlooks a lovely garden with green shrubs, flowers, and some large trees providing shade. We lunch on the pleasant and natural patio. My quiche tastes bland, but the salad and bread make up for it, not to mention the chocolate mousse afterward. One of the women asks if we will share our pictures of the Pope with her friend who is a devout Catholic. Embarrassed, we have to fess up our pictures only show the limo the Pope rides in. We forgot to tell her earlier it was sort of a joke between us. The pictures of the limo only show black windows. The laughing soldiers were right. We could not actually see the Pope in the darkened bulletproof limo. Our friend looks disappointed. The conversation turns to all the stairs on the streets of the Old City. I complain my knees don't do well on the steps. Our friend tells us all the ladies working down in the souk wrap their knees with cabbage leaves. I feel like I just won the lottery. We'll try it when we get back to the Gloria. If it works in the Old City, it will work anywhere.

After a long lunch we saunter down toward the busy street and happen upon a little place called the Psalms Museum. It turns out to be quite a find. The artist himself explains his interpretations of the Psalms in brush stroke and color. The Museum of Psalms reflects one man's work. He takes the seven shekel donation, explains his paintings, and answers any questions. God gave this Jew the vision and desire to create a work of art for each of the one hundred fifty Psalms. He uses distinctive colors to represent things like hope, faith, and love. He has a style all his own. The paintings, all accompanied by Scripture verses, cover the walls. As we leisurely enjoy the art, the resident cat begins attacking my cane like a dangling string. Enjoying the game, I tease her by dragging the tip as we move down the hall. As usual, the outside of this building gave no clue as to what we were getting into.

I end up buying a couple of small prints. We taxi to the Church of all Nations. This beautifully decorated church represents many countries and reminds me that our God rules the nations. He is the ruler of all the nations. When they all truly acknowledged that fact, by more than a few designs on a ceiling, the world will be a better place.

David goes to the front of the sanctuary, approaching the Rock of Agony surrounded by stylized thorns in wrought iron as a reminder of the torture Christ suffered. This may be the actual rock where Jesus sweats blood. David kneels here and prays, *Thank You Lord, for what You did for me on the cross and for the agony you suffered here making the decision to obey. Thank You for taking on my sins and offering the perfect sacrifice even though it meant you would be tortured and beaten and nailed to on a cross. Clearly You knew the suffering about to commence and yet You loved me enough to proceed and yield to the Father's will. I am overwhelmed by gratitude. I don't know if I could have stayed awake and prayed like you asked the disciples to do. I probably would have fallen asleep like Peter did. I'm sorry You had to go through that alone. You deserve so much better from all Your disciples including me.* This place creates a meaningful moment to thank Jesus for obeying the Father, even when He didn't want to.

After his blessed time of prayer, David confers with the monk on duty at the sanctuary. I sit in a back pew observing all the people, the paintings on the walls and ceiling, and the rock in the front of the sanctuary. I'm focused on that rock when David says we should go outside. David goes to find the gatekeeper for the secret garden. This garden remains so secret I know nothing about any of this. A lot of noise and dirt fly around outside the Church of all Nations because of construction. Finally I see David speaking with a man who might be the gatekeeper. I hear the man say, "No, it's impossible," and leave. A minute later the man reappears, producing an antique gate key. He takes us across the street to an ornate dark steel gate in a stone wall. He uses the key to open the heavy gate. David and I step into the secret garden.

The gatekeeper locks the door behind us and leaves. The secret garden hides us from the tourist confusion and construction noise. The official "Garden of Gethsemane" across the street displays ancient olive trees, said to be 2,000 years old. In 1999, you could wander freely among those trees. Now they hide behind protective fences. You can walk past and view the olive trees that Jesus walked under and may have prayed under. They no longer allow tourists to go near or touch those olive trees.

The secret garden offers neatly groomed gravel paths with blooming flowers here and there. It feels more like a place Jesus came for solitude and prayers, and less like a tourist attraction. For the next half hour, we soak up the luxury of roaming alone among the ancient olive trees. A sign on the stone wall says *Gethsemane*. We find a marble bench and sit down to pray for the next 20 minutes. What Christian could ever forget the night Jesus asked His disciples if they could pray with Him for one hour? They fell asleep. He went on to pray. He prayed the agonizing prayer, *"If it be*

Your will, let this cup pass from Me." The sweat from his brow turned to blood while the disciples slept. Jesus, a man who knew no sin, wrestled with the prophesied events to come.

The gate to the Secret Garden.

He chose to pay the price for my sin. He endured the cross, and then rose again, defying death itself. I throw myself on His mercy. Taking the time to sit, pray, and reflect on the happenings in this place brings my spirit a peace, the peace that comes only from Him. The secret garden, a momentous experience, brings me close to my Savior once again. The gatekeeper appears and unlocks the gate. I peek back through the decorative iron gate, saying good-bye to the ancient olive trees, those craggy witnesses of things long ago.

Ancient olive trees in the Secret Garden.

We tell the taxi appearing in front of us to take us to the top of the Mount of Olives. He cheerfully obliges. From here we view the entire Temple Mount and the Old City, an awesome sight! A camel waits at the top of the Mount of Olives. I have no intention of getting on him. Try telling that to my husband and two crazy Arabs! They literally pick me up and set me on the camel's back. The camel gets up (by the way, camels are tall). I keep saying softly, so as to not upset the camel, "Get me down from here. I want off." They take my picture and the camel sits down. They removed me in much the same way as they put me on.

As soon as my feet touch the ground, a young boy thrusts an olive branch at me. Not thinking, I take hold of it. The boy immediately wants money. I give him the change I have in my pocket, not much, six shekels. Now it's David's turn. Up goes the camel, pictures are taken, and the ride ends. David only has 100 shekel bills. He doesn't have any choice, so he gives the camel owner one. This causes a mob scene. Now the vendors close in to sell pictures of Jerusalem. The olive branch boy comes back for more money, sticking an olive leaf in David's pocket. Everybody wants money. The scene gets a little scary. David tells the first guy to share with his helper. We jump into the taxi. The men don't buy into the sharing deal. Vendors yell and chase us as the taxi rolls down the hill. We got our pictures. Let me just make a statement right now for future reference. I do not have to ride a camel every time I come to Israel. David can do what he wants to.

THE TWENTY-SECOND DAY

RAMPARTS – THE OTHER SIDE

"The Lord determined to tear down the wall around the Daughter of Zion. He stretched out a measuring line and did not withhold his hand from destroying. He made ramparts and walls lament; together they wasted away" (Lamentations 2:8).

The other side of the ramparts beckons us. Finishing the ramparts walk ranks high on my to-do list. Walking the ramparts represents more to me than merely the ability to walk. Besides the enormous historical and biblical representations the ramparts embody, personal growth paralleling the destruction and rebuilding of these walls make it necessary for me to conquer them. I must finish what I started. I need to walk the ramparts, not walk *just some* of the ramparts of the Old City walls. Earlier we walked the walls by the Christian and Muslim Quarters. Today we journey around the Armenian and Jewish Quarters. The other side of the ramparts is longer and said to be more difficult. I figure this side will be more fun and we will end up in the Jewish Quarter near the Western Wall.

The man selling tickets at the front gate smiles. "My name is Siade. You know what that means? Happy!"

"You seem happy," I smile back.

"Yes, madam," he kisses my hand and shakes David's. David's considers Siade a little too happy. With tickets in hand, we descend the first set of stairs so we can ascend the long sets of iron spiral staircases ahead. I think to myself, *oh, this is such a piece of cake.* Up the first three sets I count, *fourteen per set, just like at home, from the basement. Nope. It's eighteen. Nope. It's ....* The final set of stairs gets me. Four flights up on a rusty landing I make the mistake of looking down and freeze. This section hangs in mid air. A rusty catwalk attaches the circular stairway to the wall six feet away. My situation seems akin to balancing on a steel girder three stories up. I can't do it. I stop, "David, I don't think I can do this. I can't do it." I keep looking down, even though I desperately want to look away. Unable to tear my eyes from the drop below, panic sets in. I clutch the handrail. My adrenalin kicks in.

My heart races. I can't breathe. *Yes, breathe, breathe.* Finally I begin taking long gasping breaths. I glance up momentarily, then back down, weighing the prospect of descending the stairs. No way! I remind myself to look up, not down. *Lord, please relax me so I can function.* I must get up the stairs spiraling above my head. It seems like minutes, but probably only seconds pass. I can't move.

Behind me, David asks if it would help if he goes on ahead of me. I whimper, "I think so." I have to back down a step and stand on the catwalk to let him by, shaking the whole time.

Up to the Ramparts — a piece of cake.

He goes on up, then yells back, "If it helps any, there's a smooth floor up here and shade." I suck a deep breath and begin stepping up and up and up, too terrified even to count. Once at the top, I fall against the solid stone wall. I want to hug that solid wall. I bend over to catch my breath. David gives me a drink. I can't look back down those stairs. They drained the arrogance right out of me!

Once past that treacherous experience, the weather looks cooperative for a ramparts walk. Recovering from the steps episode, I begin to enjoy walking far above the city taking lots of pictures. The King David Hotel, such a historic landmark in Jerusalem, looks more majestic from the ramparts than from our hotel dining room. We stroll between high fortified walls with occasional spaces for viewing. An adjacent roof top patio presents a group of musicians playing about twenty different instruments and a man reading out of the Bible. "Why do the nations rage?" He man preaches out of Psalm 2. "In this case, we could say why does the United Nations rage?" An interpreter translates the preacher's English into another language (not Hebrew). They protest the UN and pray for Israel to remain true to God. We witness watchmen on the ramparts praying for the peace of Jerusalem.

We praise God for believers walking the walls with their Bibles. We take a few pictures and move on to the first tower. The plaque identifies this as a Jordanian Military Position. I remember seeing the same thing when we walked the other side of the ramparts. Jordanian snipers controlled this walk and the Old City until 1967. Another plaque explains, "The stone wall on the left, built by soldiers of the Jordanian Arab Legion after 1948, combined with the wall on the right to form a communicating trench between the various military positions. The original metal roof and thick overlying layer of sand were removed after 1967." Once again, we traverse set after set of ancient stone steps, usually knee high. Praise God, no more steel spiral stairs hang in mid air! I look down over the side, observing the road to Jerusalem University College and the tricky intersection we crossed each day on the way to class in 1998.

The wall's tower plaque reports that "the ruined stones and remains of walls between them are remnants of the fortifications of Jerusalem in various periods; the Second Temple Period, the Byzantine period and the Arab and Crusader periods." Our journey continues past another tower and then by the Yemin Moshe and Mishkenot Sha'anani neighborhoods.

The sign reports, "West of Sultan's Pool is a residential neighborhood, dominated by a windmill. Philanthropist Moses Montefiore built the first houses there for the first Jews living outside the walls. After the War of Independence in 1948, the neighborhood became a slum, because of its proximity to the border. It was renovated and reconstructed after the Six-Day War in 1967 and became one of Jerusalem's most sought after neighborhoods." The Six-Day War changed a lot of things around here. World class urban planners labored to create a city of neighborhoods meeting the needs of students, tourists, archaeologists, politicians, and families. Once again Jerusalem prospers. I hope Israel never gives Jerusalem away.

A nice man with two women comes by and offers to take our picture. He snaps a couple of us resting. They move on. We let people pass us because we want to take our time and smell the roses, so to speak. The Southwestern Citadel looms ahead. The plaque reads, "The southwestern corner tower in the Ottoman wall is built over the remains of a large fortress that dated back to the Fatimid and Crusader periods. The remains may be seen at the foot of an outside tower."

The musicians catch up to us. We find a shady nitch in which to sit while they march past. In strange accents, they say "Hi," smiling and nodding as they go by. One fellow carries a large shofar coiled around a tall walking staff. As he passes by, David asks him, "Will you blow your shofar for us?" The entire group stops. The man graciously grants David's request. The sight of this man raising the shofar above the walls of Jerusalem thrills us. The powerful sound blowing across the city takes me back centuries, to the time of Jesus, and then flashes forward to the future when the prophesied trumpet sounds. I catch my breath at the spirituality of the moment.

We raise our hands and yell, "Hallelujah, praise the Lord!" His tour group joins our praises. Behind him his friend sticks out his hand saying, "We're from Germany. Where are you from?" Jerusalem draws people from every corner of the world. "Where are you from?" It's the question everyone asks. He smiles, "You must be Christians." We shake his hand and the group marches on past us. Each one takes time to say "thank you" and "bless you" as they go by, another special moment.

Continuing our ramparts walk, we reach Domitian Abbey. The German Catholics of the Benedictines built the bell tower and church building

in the second half of the 19th century (not so old). This church marks the traditional place the Virgin Mary fell into a deep sleep. We continue past another guard room. The musicians from Germany receive another sermon on this historic spot. I gaze across the city at the big gold dome. On the south side of the wall we draw near the end of our rampart walk. Here at Gallicantu, Jesus' disciple, Peter, denied Christ three times, just as Jesus predicted. A little farther down the path, we pass a park built inside the wall. It features ping-pong tables, picnic tables, shade trees, a basketball court, jungle gym, a tot lot type area, and other things. They stand vacant. I wonder why no families enjoy this lovely park today. The turnstile ahead signals the end of the ramparts walk. David sets the camera to get our picture – hats and canes held high, we pose – victory!

Off the ramparts, into the Jewish Quarter, we search for refreshment. The Cardo comes into view. David and I snack on cokes and pizza. Tonight Shavuot[47] begins! The Jewish Quarter prepares to celebrate. In addition, groups of tourists abound in a sea of confusion. The Old City gets more crowded as the day wears on. David and I decide to catch a museum or two

---

47 Shavuot (or Shavuos) is a Jewish festival commemorating the revelation at Sinai and the giving of the Torah. Many Jews celebrate by staying up all night studying Torah.

before the festivities begin. We wander over to Burnt House. We arrive in time to see them closing. We go over to the Temple Institute. It's closed, too. Evidently, the holiday celebration starts now. The Four Sephardic Synagogues draw us back.

We started to visit them earlier in the day, but were distracted by Esther Weiss' Hat Shop. There, after much trying on, David got me a gorgeous hat. Esther showed me how Jewish women tie their headscarves, so he got me some of them, too. Thrilled with my new knowledge, I wore one out of the store. I tell this now because when we get to the Four Sephardic Synagogues, my head covering and David's kippa makes us look Jewish. David thinks we get a more personal tour because of it. I don't know. I stand out as one of only a few women wearing pants, not counting tourists. You don't walk the ramparts in a dress!

The Four Sephardic Synagogues endured an interesting history of suffering, faith, and rebirth. Because of their low profile, this synagogue, out of fifty-two in the Jewish Quarter, stands today as the only one not destroyed by the Jordanians in 1948. The Four Sephardic Synagogues sounds plural, yet can be interpreted as singular. The information from *Jerusalem Footsteps Through Time* describes the history of these (or this) still active synagogue.

The Sephardic community in Jerusalem began as early as the Ramban, but its significant population growth and its independent character came with the traumatic jolt of 1492 – the Spanish expulsion. Jews evicted from Spain and Portugal and looking for a place to live moved around the Turkish Empire – Turkey, Bulgaria, and Greece – where they were welcomed by the Turkish rulers. In 1517, the Ottoman Empire conquered the Land of Israel, and its gates were opened to Jews, many of whom made it their home. Those who arrived in Jerusalem found a community of Ashkenazim and mistaravim (native Jews), who all prayed together in the Ramban Synagogue. When this place of worship was expropriated in 1586 by the mufti of Jerusalem, Abu Seifan ("owner of the two swords"), the Sephardim moved south to build their own synagogue. They soon became the majority among the Jews in the city. The first synagogues they built were Kahal Kadosh Talmud Torah (Eliyahu HaNavi) and the Kahal Kadosh Gadol (Rabban Yochanan ben Zakai) at the end of the sixteenth century. The Middle and Istanbuli synagogues were later additions (1720-1740) to the growing community.

It is not clear how the Jews received permission to construct synagogues, considering the prohibitive Covenant of Omar. Possibly Suleiman the Magnificent himself, who favored the Jews, allowed it. Still, synagogues were built low, since Islamic laws prevented Jewish buildings from towering over Muslim institutions. The Jews had to submit to this decree even though, halachically[48], a synagogue is to occupy the highest spot in the city.

Ottoman goodwill did not last long. By the second half of the eighteenth century, the synagogues were in terrible condition. The roofs had fallen in, and, on rainy days, worshippers were soaked to the bone. But the Arabs would not agree to repairs. Only with the Egyptian occupation of Jerusalem in 1835 did the Jews receive permission from Ibrahim Pasha to renovate.

Interestingly, when the authorities finally acquiesced, halachic difficulties further delayed renovation. Rabbi Shlomo Moshe Suzin, the Sephardic chief rabbi, enforced the law that no synagogue may be dismantled before its replacement is built. However, the gabbim (sextons) had the upper hand, and the old synagogues were restored first. They then became the center of Jerusalem's Sephardic Jewry.

The Rabban Yochanan ben Zakai Synagogue

The most impressive of the four synagogues was the Rabban Yochanan ben Zakai Synagogue (also called Kahal Kadosh Gadol – el Kahal Grande). Legend has it that on this spot stood the beit midrash (study hall) of the great Second Temple Sage Rabban Yochanan ben Zakai. Visiting Jews considered receiving an aliyah [Torah reader] here a great honor, since this is believed to be the earliest and most important of the four. (However, an architectural survey seems to indicate that Eliyahu HaNavi Synagogue came first.) The design is characteristically Sephardic, with the seats facing the center, whereas in Ashkenazic synagogues they face the front. The Rabban Yochanan

---

48 According to Jewish religious law.

ben Zakai Synagogue may have originally been modeled after the Ramban synagogue – it, too, had a row of columns down the middle that held up a wooden roof. The design might explain why there are two aronot kodesh[holy arks that store the Torah scrolls] in the front of the synagogue – the dividing columns left no available center. However, multiple aronot [arks] are found in other synagogues as well. Perhaps the origin of the practice is the tradition that the Jews, in Biblical times, had two arks. One was taken out to war and the second remained in the Tabernacle's Holy of Holies (Jerusalem Talmud). Or, double arks may have stemmed from an unpleasant tradition, born in Buchara, where the Islamic authorities forced the Jews to keep a Koran in the synagogue. To avoid storing the Koran together with the Holy Torah, two separate aronot were built.

With the renovation of the synagogue in 1835, the columns and wooden roofs were removed and replaced with arched vaults. Notice that the Jewish builders integrated their beliefs into the architecture by having the arches meet at a circle, the center of which forms two tablets. They avoided the classic Gothic arch, which would have formed a cross on the ceiling. All the current fittings in the synagogue as well as the aronot are new. The old furniture and paintings were burned in the War of Independence. The previous decorations on the front wall (Mizrach) display the Kotel on the right and the Me'arat HaMachpelah, the Cave of the Partiarchs, on the left. These covered up an earlier decoration that caused heated controversy in the Sephardic community.

Rabbi Mordecai Shnitzer, a renowned sculptor and one of the ten disciples of the Vilna Gaon who moved from Safed to Jerusalem at the beginning of the century, was contracted by the gabbaim [similar to a deacon]of the Sephardic community to build the aronot kodesh. He did so, and decorated the wall above with a pair of lions holding up the Ten Commandments from either side, as was customary in Eastern European synagogues. But the Chief Sephardic Rabbi Shlomo Moshe Suzin disapproved of having animal figures in the synagogue. The gabbaim, who had received the permit to renovate and had invested more than one million paisters to rebuild it into a house

172

of prayer for a thousand people, felt they, too, had a say. But this time the rabbi laid down the law and the lions were removed.

The yearning for redemption took on a tangible form in the Sephardic community. Atop the southern wall (to your right), you can see a shofar and a flask of oil, replacing those that stood there for many years. The shofar is to be blown by the prophet Elijah upon the arrival of the Messiah. The oil is to be used to anoint the Messianic King himself (or for the ner tamid – the eternal lamp). The members of the community never touch these holy objects. These Jews were sure the Messiah would be anointed in their synagogue, which they saw as a center of Jewish life. Synagogue tradition tells of a secret tunnel that led from here to the Temple Mount, facilitating the completion of the Messiah's journey. The synagogue even replicated one of the Temple's miracles – with thousands crowding it on the festivals, no one ever complained of lack of space.

The Rabbi Yochanan ben Zakai Synagogue was the Sephardic center of Jewish life in Jerusalem. All important community ceremonies took place here. One of these was the appointment of the Sephardic chief rabbi, the rishon leTzion, who was recognized by the Ottoman authorities as the Jewish Chacham Bashi, a powerful office of leadership. (Indeed, Sephardim – not Ashkenazim – were the only authentic Jews in the eyes of the Ottoman Empire.) Another key event occurred in the synagogue in 1870 when a reception was held for the Austrian Kaiser, Franz Josef.

The Eliyahu HaNavi Synagogue

Scholars claim that this was the earliest synagogue of the complex, even though the community book of regulations gives this honor to the Rabban Yochanan ben Zakai Synagogue. The synagogue was previously known as Kahal Kadosh Talmud Torah, and served as both a house of prayer and a study hall. Later, when the metivta (yeshiva) was built, it became the main study hall.

The name Eliyahu HaNavi (Elijah the Prophet) was adopted following an unusual occurrence. The Jewish community had dwindled to the extent there were no longer ten adult males for a minyan. The community was especially distraught about conducting Yom Kippur services with only nine men. On the eve of Yom Kippur, however, just before Kol Nidrei, a tenth Jew appeared, dressed in white and exuding a special aura. The delighted community went about the Yom Kippur prayers with extra zeal and exaltation. At the end of the day, the congregants all gathered around this special person who had honored them with his presence. They wanted to thank him and invite him to break the fast with them. But the man refused and asked permission to complete his prayers in a small adjoining room. (This room is just to the north, down a few steps.) As time passed, and he did not emerge, they went to see what had happened – and found the room empty. The tenth man had vanished into thin air. They then realized they had prayed that Yom Kippur with Elijah the prophet. The synagogue was named after him, and a marble sign above this small room said, "This is where Elijah the Prophet, of blessed memory, was revealed." His chair (kisei Eliyahu) was placed inside the room and adorned with embroidered garments. On it, the community's children entered into the covenant of Abraham. (The chair, like the rest of the synagogue's furniture, disappeared in 1948.)

Another story is told of a blood libel planned by Christians. They concealed a dead baby in this synagogue in order to bring false charges against the Jews, but Rabbi Klonimus used God's name to revive the infant. To commemorate the miracle, a stone inscribed with that holy name was kept in the aron kodesh. The aron you see here is not the original but was brought from a synagogue in Livorno, Italy. This sixteenth-century antique aron kodesh is one of the oldest remaining Sephardic aronot kodesh and it stood in the main synagogue of Livorno until the latter was destroyed in the Second World War. The survivors of that dwindling Jewish community donated their aron to this synagogue, linking their past with the future of Jerusalem.

The Middle Synagogue: Kahal Katan (Kahal Medio) – Kahal Tzion

The expanding Sephardic community of the eighteenth century outgrew its synagogue, and the overflow established a second minyan in the women's section. This quorum eventually developed into a new synagogue, incorporating part of the courtyard. The women, who until then had prayed in the courtyard, moved up to the gallery. The name Middle Synagogue came later, when the place found itself sandwiched between the new Istanbuli and the Rabban Yochanan ben Zakai Synagogues. The original name was Kahal Tzion, because an underground tunnel supposedly connected this synagogue to the "Tomb of David" on Mount Zion.

The Middle Synagogue copied the basic design of the mother synagogue, the Rabban Yochanan ben Zakai – a long room with round arches. Note the pyramid-shaped windows in the western wall. Light enters them from the open courtyard (where a sukkah was built).

Below the windows, interesting stone-cut decorations (a square and a circle) surround the entrance. According to an old Moroccan custom, the tombstones of males are decorated with circles, and those of females feature squares. It is unknown what place this symbolism has in the synagogue. The aron kodesh is from eighteenth-century Piedmont, Italy. This synagogue was renovated in 1835 and again in 1967, like its neighbors, but today it is not in use.

The Istanbuli Synagogue

The last of the four synagogues to be built was the Istanbuli, constructed in 1764 by immigrants from Istanbul. It is patterned after the Eliyahu HaNavi Synagogue, only much bigger. Unlike the other synagogues, this one has no legend attaching it to a specific group. Maybe that is why it attracted the working class of different edot (ethnic groups). Here, shopkeepers and artisans from Eastern communities – Kurdistan, North and West Africa – came to pray. Underneath the synagogue lies an ancient water cistern used for tashlich (a ritual in which Jews symbolically cast their sins into a body of water on the first day of Rosh Hashanah). Above the square column in the prayer hall is an oval, framed, partially damaged inscription giving the date of the synagogue's renovation as 5596 (1836). However, above the entrance, the inscription states: "This is the Gate of God, our Lord. May He redeem Zion and rebuild the cities of Judea....Enter His gates with thanks – 5595 (1835)."

The original doorway, which leads to Beit El Street, is closed on weekdays. On the other side of this entrance (from Beit El Street) is a beautiful set of doors with intricate, ornamental stone cuts. The furnishings of the Istanbuli, like those in the other synagogues, have been imported from abandoned prayer centers in Italy. This aron kodesh dates back to the seventeenth century and presided over an Ancona synagogue destroyed years ago. Note the fine, wooden engravings gilded in gold. Inside the two doors of the aron are the tablets of the law, and the top of the ark bears the inscription "Keter Torah (crown of Torah). The bimah [elevated platform] comes from a synagogue in Pesaro. At its bottom you can see how its eighteenth century craftsmen imagined the Temple. The bimah stands today against the western wall, as it did in the synagogue in Pesaro, although the original Istanbuli bimah stood in the center, as in the other Sephardic synagogues.

Epilogue

When the Arab Legion broke through the Jewish defenders' lines in 1948, the four synagogues were used as a giant shelter for the Quarter's residents. The low buildings protected the 1,500 residents of the Old City from the shells and bullets of the Arabs. On Friday, May 28, 1948, the Jewish Quarter surrendered. The synagogues were occupied by the Arabs, and the old furnishings brought by the Jews from Spain – and religious artifacts such as the shofar and the flask of oil – disappeared. The buildings themselves, though scarred, remained intact; after the Six-Day War, the Sephardic community renovated them. Today, once again, they serve as houses of prayer and Torah study.[49]

This amazing story makes our visit to the Four Sephardic Synagogues one of the highlights of our stay in the Old City. We move on to Hurva Square and grab a cool seat in front of a shaded general store. David buys ice cream. Scores of people make their way through the square preparing for a celebration. Families, groups of teens, school groups, and Jews visiting Israel just for this holiday congregate in the square. A motorcycle with a four foot tall oscillating fan strapped onto the back

---

49 Reprinted from *Jerusalem Footsteps through Time* with permission of Feldheim Publishers.

stops at a Yeshiva (school) nearby to unload. A van squeezes by, topped by no less than a dozen thin mattresses. Crammed inside the van are people, camping equipment, and who knows what else jostling side to side. The driver attempts the impossible. They don't get far past the first turn. But no matter, everyone tumbles out, picking up gear, and walking. The mood escalates with joyous expectation.

More fans arrive accompanied by food and cases of water. Local synagogues obviously plan on lots of guests inside the walls tonight. People shop for flowers. The air of anticipation for Shavuot increases. Christian tour groups pass by taking pictures, buying souvenirs and consuming snacks. Oblivious to the preparations for Shavuot, they continue on their standard "Old City" tour.

"This reminds me of what the second coming of Christ will be like," David muses. "The Scriptures say it will be like in the days of Noah. People will be eating and drinking, working, and living their everyday ordinary lives – just like when it started to rain. The people didn't expect that day to be any different from any other day." I agree whole-heartedly. David goes on, "This makes me think. This could be the day! Wow! The righteous Jews will be up studying Torah all night. Elijah could show up at the Sephardic Synagogue and blow the shofar. Jesus could descend on the Mount of Olives just as the righteous Jews make their way to the Wall at sunrise. The day He comes will be just like this afternoon. This could be the day!"

Matthew 24:36-39 supports what David says, *"No one knows about that day or hour, not even the angels in heaven, nor the Son, but only the Father. As it was in the days of Noah, so it will be at the coming of the Son of Man. For in the days before the flood, people were eating and drinking, marrying and giving in marriage, up to the day Noah entered the ark; and they knew nothing about what would happen until the flood came and took them all away. That is how it will be at the coming of the Son of Man."*

In the meantime, we witness the never ending confusion of a tiny one lane street in Jerusalem's Old City. A one way street, the one way depends on which way you want to go. Should a police van, or something bigger, come face to face with you, the one way changes to whatever way they want to go!

Refreshed, we start back to the Gloria. I remind David to buy cabbage if we see a place. I want to test that little hint about knees and cabbage.

A grocery appears at the turn above the Cardo. David comes out with cabbage and pecans. We hurry to St. James Church, open only from 3 – 3:40 pm. We barely make it by 3:30. Closed again, they have shortened their hours by ten minutes. They celebrate Ascension Day today. They went to the Mount of Olives. Today the church isn't even open for the half hour. I doubt we get inside this important site in the Armenian Quarter on this trip.

In Biblical times faithful Jews, including Jesus and the disciples, journeyed to the Temple in Jerusalem to celebrate the three festivals required by God in Exodus 23:14. For Shavuot, the Festival of the First Fruits, farmers brought God the first kernels of the wheat harvest. Shavuot also marks the anniversary of the day God gave the Torah to Moses and the Israelites at Mt. Sinai. Jews value God's laws as a gift rather than a burden. Shavuot follows Passover. Passover celebrates the passing over of the Israelites by the "destroyer of the first-born" and their deliverance from Egypt.

God parted the Red Sea and the *"people passed through as on dry land, but when the Egyptians passed through, they were drowned."* The Torah mandates the seven-week counting of the Omer, beginning on the 2nd day of Passover, for 50 days, immediately followed by Shavuot. In the Bible, Shavuot is called the Festival of Weeks. Counting the Omer for 50 days reminds Jews of the connection between Passover and Shavuot. Passover celebrates the gift of God's laws that redeemed Israel from spiritual bondage and idolatry. Christians celebrate the same holiday as Pentecost, fifty days after Easter. On that day, the disciples received the Holy Spirit and some 3,000 Hebrews got saved in Jerusalem. This connection between Old and New Testaments, between Jew and Christian, comforts me.

Back at the hotel, I'm trying to figure out how to tie cabbage leaves around my aching knees. Frustrated, I write in my journal for a few hours before tackling that task again. It's getting late and I am ready to call it a day. We've been invited to a friend's home for Erev Shabbat tomorrow. I look forward to celebrating Shabbat with friends. I plan to wash my hair tomorrow afternoon, nothing else. Then David drops a little bomb. The guide at the Four Sephardic Synagogues invited us to return tonight and join them for Shavuot Torah studies. He tells me he will get up at 2:30 a.m., get dressed, and leave the hotel at 3:00 a.m. to go to the Sephardic

Synagogue to pray. At sunrise he will go to the wall. This news did not fall upon agreeable ears or knees.

Considerate and understanding, David wouldn't ask me to get up at 2:30 a.m. He correctly assumes I prefer to sleep in. I seethe inside. My anger reflects my fears. I'm afraid for him, *oh, great; he's going to be running around the streets of Jerusalem at 3:00 in the morning. There are lots of soldiers with guns out there. Anything could happen.* I try to talk him out of it, but he is adamant. *OK, so I don't go and he gets shot. How long will it take for them to find me? How am I going to ship his body back to Colorado? I'd better go. Maybe I could even help him or call for a doctor. It will be better than sitting here waiting for bad news.* "O.K., I'll go," I sigh. My brilliant husband knows getting up at 2:30 a.m. doesn't appeal to me.

"No, I don't want you to go if you don't really want to go because it won't be good," he wisely answers. I can't imagine trying to worship with my present attitude.

"OK, I want to go. I'm praying about my attitude in this," I feel I have no choice but to insist on going along, even though I dread it. I wash my hair, pack my little bag, and retie the cabbage on my knees with strips made from cutting the plastic grocery bag. I try to hum a happy little tune while getting ready for bed. Oh, how I want to sleep, knowing in a few short hours the alarm will go off. Exasperation confounds my attempts to sleep. Every time I move my cabbage wrapped knees, those darn shopping bag strips crinkle loudly, breaking the silence of the night, and waken me. I'm so tired. *Does cabbage really help your knees?* I'm beginning to wonder if my friend, disappointed in not getting pictures of the Pope, decided to play a little joke on me. Finally, around 10:30 p.m., I abandon the cabbage leaf treatment for a few hours sleep!

THE TWENTY-THIRD DAY

SHAVUOT

"On the day of first fruits, when you present to the Lord an offering of new grain during the Feast of Weeks, hold a sacred assembly and do no regular work" (Numbers 28:26).

My eyes open and focus on the sleeping alarm clock, 2:25 a.m. *Actually,* I think, *I feel pretty good.* Praise God, I can function at this hour. Choosing what to wear today, I decide my pink print top has black flowers and works with the black skirt. My new pink hat and scarf make me feel like a little Jewish lady getting ready for synagogue. David wears his white shirt and black pants complete with suspenders and kippa. Unfortunately, I can't bring myself to wear the white walking shoes I brought for slogging through Hezekiah's tunnel and end up wearing most days. I cave to vanity and wear the cute black sandals. Anxiety sweeps through my spirit about going into the streets of Jerusalem at 3:00 a.m. *Fear keeps us from doing too many things,* I reason with myself. I begin asking God to strengthen me and renew my resolve to do this without kvetching all the way. Participation in this celebration means something to David.

I contemplate the long trudge down to the Sephardic Synagogues in the dark! David is ready. We step out of the Gloria courtyard. I look apprehensively down to Jaffa Road. Surprisingly, I see people roaming to and fro. Mothers push baby strollers with toddlers following. Groups of women and girls walk alone. Couples stroll on well lit streets. Soldiers patrol. Down at Jaffa Road we see many Orthodox and Hassidic Jewish men and women. A few people wear jeans. We see some women wearing pants. The Old City pulsates with Jewish activity. With no cars around, pedestrians fill the streets all the way to the synagogue. We see more soldiers. When we get to the synagogue, I become a problem. When we toured here earlier, I failed to check out how to get up to the women's area. I did see their balcony above where the men meet. We peek into the glass door. Only men sit around a large table, studying. David says, "Let's go in and ask."

"I can't go in there," I step back into the shadows.

A women's loft in the Sephardic Synagogues.

David enters to discretely find how to get me upstairs. The rabbi teaches a lesson in Hebrew. By 3:30 a.m., some at the table have their heads down and others stretch their legs and drink coffee. David quietly whispers to a man standing nearest the door, asking how to get upstairs. The man doesn't understand English or can't hear. Next, David asks a young student who understands English, but has no idea how to get upstairs. He asks another man, who stops the lesson and asks the rabbi! David succeeds in disrupting the entire room. So much for being discrete! The rabbi tells David to go outside and up a flight of stairs. When we arrive around the corner we find a locked door.

A group of teenaged girls wait for their rabbi to lead them to their next synagogue tonight. The young girls talk and giggle. The mood feels light, in spite of, or maybe because of, the hour. We follow them to the Eliahu Hanaui Talmud Torah Congregation. The helpful rabbi tells us seating is "mixed," meaning men and women can sit together. Anyway, that's what I thought it meant. After sitting a few minutes, I understood that "mixed" means both sexes can sit on the same level. Fortunately, David and I sat near the middle of the room. David sits beside me on the women's side, but only a few inches from the men. We quickly shed our jackets. The packed room is hot in spite of fans struggling to bring in the cool night air. My first time at a synagogue service, I have high expectations.

The speaker, Rabbi David Aaron, speaks about what it means to be Jewish and whole. Several times he says, "We are not God, we are one with God." Yes, I agree. Then he says, "They say Yeshua was God, but He was not and He was not the Messiah." Suddenly we feel alone and rejected along with our Messiah. Immediately I go into prayer mode. Even though John 4:22 proclaims *"salvation is from the Jews,"* we know most Jews don't recognize Yeshua as their Messiah. We didn't think it would come up tonight because tonight is about Moses and the Ten Commandments. I'm saddened for those sitting around me. These are God's chosen people yet they don't see His gift of salvation through Yeshua. It hurts me deeply because I love Him and I love them. God reminds me of two very important truths. Many times Yeshua stood in front of congregations in synagogues like this, and so did Paul and the disciples. I was once an enemy of God's, but through Yeshua I've become reconciled to God. Again I remember the Scripture in Romans 11:26-29, *"And so all Israel will be saved, as it is written: 'The deliverer will come from Zion; he will turn godlessness away from Jacob. And this is my covenant with them when I take away their sins. As far as the gospel is concerned, they are enemies on your account; but as far as election is concerned, they are loved on account of the patriarchs, for God's gifts and his call are irrevocable."* My mood brightens and I feel encouraged as I remember God's extraordinary plan for these faithful Jews.

David Aaron describes what the Messiah will be like – a man who embodies the goodness and fullness of God. Jesus did all that and much more, such as, miracles, and fulfilling prophecy. God Himself testified about Jesus at His baptism and, oh yes, He resurrected people from death, including Himself. There could be no clearer proof of God's temporary blinding of the Jewish people than this back to back denial and statement of Messianic expectation.

Aaron mentions the Talmud, but surprisingly never mentions the laws of Moses (Ten Commandments). God's gift of His Law constitutes the reason for this holiday. Aaron only refers to them as a passing reference to mitzvot, which sounds more like doing good deeds than obeying the 613 laws in the Torah. He hypes his own books and seminars on this holy night reserved for God's Book. In closing, he spells his name for us, A-a-r-o-n. Apparently, among the stay up all night and study Torah crowd, he expects many would not be able to spell Aaron. It only proves that kings who conquer enemies are more popular than the original high priest, Moses' brother, Aaron! He doesn't spell David for the group, just Aaron.

He stands up after his presentation. David and I sit there, as the room gets noisy. People begin to mill around, visit, and take down chairs. A few minutes later we creep up to the empty loft and open David's Bible. David confesses feeling the need to pray up here in the quiet. We take turns reading Psalms 119. As we take turns reading, the Lord restores us. Afterward, we feel ready to go to the Wall. We return to the streets, joining the crowds streaming to the Wall. Now everyone hurries. Dawn approaches. No need to rush, the Kotel Plaza crowd arrived earlier. I head down the steps at full clip, not aware David has a difficult time keeping up because of his sore knee. He must take each step down with his good knee. Right now he stands in awe of the cabbage leaf cure! Little does he know I abandoned that gig early in the evening!

Staircases down to security flow with men, women, and children. I start pulling off my bag and camera for security check. Security waves us

Shavuot crowds at the Western Wall.

through. No time for inspections now. The plaza transforms into a sea of people mostly wearing black. David holds up his camera taking a few pictures of the crowd. A young Israeli girl, perhaps about twenty years old, starts yelling at him in Hebrew. I get the words, "Yom kodesh," but not the rest. *Yom is day. Kodesh is holy. Holy day.* She shouts angrily, "Shavuot." She says that Shavuot is a holy day. No pictures! David puts his camera away. Thousands gather here. The partitions dividing the men and women's sides extend almost entirely across the plaza.

As we talk, David realizes he stands in the women's area! We back off until we join more men in the mix. The sun rises, incredibly changing the scene. The early glow of the sun reflects off ancient stones surrounding us. From shadows to light, the crowded Kotel teems with prayers and conversation. We find seats near the exit. We're not supposed to sit here, but the guards don't bother us. They shoo other people away from the precious sitting space. For the next half hour we soak it all in. We wait for a shofar to blow or for people to break out in song and dance. None of that happens. People begin exiting like fans leaving a football game early. We join the crowd walking toward Jaffa Gate. The path back begins with the longest steepest hill yet. My cute black shoes drag up the hill. The tide has turned as people stream out of the city and home for breakfast. What an unforgettable morning!

Our route takes us by St. James Church. We stop in, trying to catch the morning service. We think it was 6 – 6:30 a.m.. Now 6:00 a.m., the doors stand closed. No morning service, just open 3 – 3:30 p.m. A local woman taught us to shrug our shoulders and say, "Because this is Jerusalem!" The Gloria beckons.

Back in our room, I rest. Later we go up to breakfast. Most patrons act oblivious to the Shavuot holiday. Four men at a table next to us know about it and mention that the younger group went down to check it out. That would be us! Yes, us with our canes. Canes become a normal part of life for many because of all the steps and cobblestones. It doesn't mark you as old or give you much extra space or consideration – because it's Jerusalem!

David brings Shawarmas with Pepsi Max for lunch from Four Brothers restaurant. I fall asleep. Soon it's early afternoon. Time to go to our friend's home for Erev Shabbat! Our driver struggles with her address, but a cell phone call helps. She lives in a friend's flat, condominium, or apartment, whatever they call it here. They have roomed together before. Her friend bought the apartment for a very good price during the 2006 Intifada. The polished Jerusalem stone steps leading to her courtyard look steep. Once we get to the courtyard, we are greeted by a lovely, spacious patio, with green vines climbing the walls and blooming flowers all around. It's like a private Garden of Eden. Today, the Holy Day of Shavuot, blends into Erev Shabbat! I love experiencing a Shabbat meal in Jerusalem. Our friend fulfills this desire for us tonight.

Four other guests represent three countries. Friends all brought food to share. Our hostess prepared the main course and dessert. She performs the traditional lighting of the candles. She welcomes the Sabbath with the Hebrew prayer, *"Baruch ata Adonai, Elohienu melech ha'olam asher kidshanu bemitzvotav vtzvanu l'hadlik ner shel shabbat. Blessed are You, Adonai our God, Ruler of the universe who has made us holy with mitzvot and commanded us to light the Sabbath candles."* David fills the wine glasses. He prays the traditional prayer over the wine, which we share from a common cup *"Baruch ata Adonai, Elohienu melech ha'olam boray pri ha-gafen. Praised are You, Adonai our God, Ruler of the universe, who creates the fruit of the vine."* We pass the cup in communion and remembrance of Yeshua, our Messiah. Then we lift our glasses and toast *"L'Chiam, to life!"* David raises the braided challah bread platter, *"Baruch ata Adonai, Elohienu melech ha'olam hamotzi lechem min ha'aretz. Blessed are You, Adonai our God, Ruler of the universe, who brings forth bread from the earth."*

We linger over delicious food and interesting stories. Conversations about the Lord and what He has done in each of our lives fills the evening. We all we love Israel and the Jews because of Yeshua. The peaceful atmosphere brings comfort. We speak of prophecy. We speak of God's plan for the world and the universe. We speak of His enduring faithfulness. One of the ladies gets very emotional voicing her love for Israel. Bridges for Peace volunteers describe how hard they work. They would love to connect with the Jewish people more personally. Often one can serve or socialize. These women come here to help. Humble service requires putting others' needs ahead of your own desires.

During our conversation, I learn something new about Jerusalem. Tarantulas live in Jerusalem! One of the ladies found two of them in her apartment. Cats abound. They sneak into apartments, too. The conversation drifts back to Bible prophecy and rather grim predictions for the United States and the world. After several moments of preaching gloom and doom, one of the ladies finishes by saying, "there is nothing for us to worry about. God promises He will take care of us."

Our hostess wants to hear about some of our Jerusalem experiences. We recount our synagogue adventures last night and going to the wall this morning. We share about the German man we met on the ramparts who blew the shofar. That scene remains indelibly stamped on my mind. It seems like we just arrived, but at 9:30 p.m. we prepare to leave. Sadly, we know won't see our friend again before returning to Colorado. We say our good-bys as our taxi arrives. We ride quietly all the way to the Gloria, each engrossed in our own thoughts.

THE TWENTY-FOURTH DAY

JERICHO

"At that time Joshua pronounced this solemn oath: 'Cursed before the Lord is the man who undertakes to rebuild this city, Jericho:' At the cost of his firstborn son will he lay its foundations; at the cost of his youngest will he set up its gates" (Joshua 6:26).

This morning buffet offers mostly bread, honey, and coffee. I finally break down and mix some fruit with yogurt and honey. Back in our room, I break out the protein snacks. Our morning revolves around the Rockefeller Museum. We missed it a couple of times earlier, so today we make it our top priority. Our taxi at Jaffa Gate wants 50 shekels for a 30 shekel ride. He makes no lower offer when David complains. We catch a taxi off the street. Everyone knows the location of the Rockefeller Museum. No buses run today because of Shabbat. In any case, God provides us with a great taxi driver, Aram. His cheerful, not pushy attitude refreshes. He points out sites along the way, like our private tour guide. We enjoy the pleasant ride. Before he drops us off, David gets his cell number just in case we need him later. Then he discloses the information that before driving a taxi, he drove a tour bus for 20 years.

The Rockefeller Museum collected items from the early years (before 1948) of archaeological excavation in the Holy Land. Artifacts uncovered in Jerusalem, Megiddo, Ashkelon, Lachish, Samaria, and Jericho flood my imagination. Stuccowork from Hisham's Palace in Jericho fills one entire large room. Another room holds 12th century marble door lintels from the Church of the Holy Sepulcher. The deep relief carving of the life of Christ overwhelms David who once tried his own hand at carving wood. Intricately carved 8th century wooden panels from Al-Aksa Mosque stand out. Lots of bones, skulls, sarcophagi, and ossuaries rest here. I love the hieroglyphics and cuneiform writings on standing stones. Tons of pottery and carved stones fill glass cases and wooden shelves. Ancient jewelry looks similar to what women wear today. I know for a fact some of those huge earrings belonged to men! John D. Rockefeller gave funds to build the museum in 1927. Designed with a courtyard in the center of the structure, the museum surrounds an oblong reflecting pool surrounded with several statuettes and a blue mosaic tiled portico. Lovely and peaceful, one can relax here between exhibits. After touring the museum, David and I sit in the courtyard musing about the history surrounding us.

The Rockefeller Museum disappoints us on a few levels. They possess lots of excellent artifacts. Without a tie in to the Bible, our interest fades. Signs explain some exhibits, however many displays have just an item number. When we try to find the item on the charts in plastic cases on the wall, they either don't answer our question or the charts have disappeared. No picture taking allowed inside. We do appreciate the free admission and benches in every area.

Aram picks us up outside the museum, expecting to take us back to Jaffa Gate. His honesty and calm spirit puts us at ease. The perfect guide for us, we decide to take advantage of the situation. We'll get some sight seeing done without killing our knees. These mark our last days here. We feel time racing by. We push on to destinations not yet visited, like St. Peter in Gallicantu. Aram begins to point out places of interest along the way. Some we already visited, some still we want to, and some we probably never will. Damascus Gate, Schindler's Tomb, the Garden Tomb, the Golden Dome Church, Dormition Abbey, the King David Hotel, the green line (between Israel and Jerusalem – pre 1967 no man's land), the hospital, and so many other sites fly by.

St. Peter in Gallicantu, a beautiful mosaic church, commemorates the traditional site where Peter fulfilled Christ's prophecy, *"Then Peter remembered the word Jesus had spoken: 'Before the rooster crows, you will disown me three times."* (Matthew 26:75). The rest of the verse says, *"And he [Peter] went outside and wept bitterly."* In Luke 22:60-62, the description of the scene is more detailed, *"Peter replied, 'Man, I don't know what you're talking about!' Just as he was speaking, the rooster crowed.* **The Lord turned and looked straight at Peter.** *Then Peter remembered the words the Lord had spoken to him: 'Before the rooster crows today you will disown me three times.' And he [Peter] went outside and wept bitterly."*

We pause for a moment inside the sanctuary. David prays a beautiful prayer for the both of us, and thanks God for His forgiveness. What a gracious God we have! We remain eternally grateful to Him for our lives and for Him.

We photograph the gorgeous mosaics on the sanctuary walls. The church, built in 1931, covers ancient caves where Christ spent the night before being taken to Pilate. We descend into the sub-basement. These caves date from the Second Temple period. Tradition places the House of Caiaphas here. Most likely, Jesus spent time imprisoned in one of these very caves. David stands in the deep cave. I snap a picture from the stairs above. He looks very small and forlorn in that dreadful place.

For a shekel you can buy a candle to place on the altar. One candle lights the entire area. By now we've become comfortable with some Catholic traditions and get two candles. We pray a short prayer of confession for letting Jesus down. We thank Him for forgiving us just as He forgave Peter for denying Him. Not only did He forgive Peter, but He gave him a powerful ministry for the rest of his life.

Outside you can still walk a Hasmonean stairway that Jesus walked. David slowly climbs the stairway and I can tell he thinks about how our Lord suffered.

Hasmonean stairway Jesus walked.

Aram waits patiently for us, even though we spend an hour at Gallicantu. As soon as we get to the taxi, he offers us cold water. What a considerate driver. One site we've neglected thus far beckons, the Kidron Valley. Aram agrees to take us. He knows all the roads and whips through Silwan to the narrow road in the Kidron Valley. The Kidron Valley separates the Old City from the Mount of Olives. It is called the Valley of Jehoshaphat in the Old Testament. This valley is of special interest to me because the Book of Joel, chapter 3, declares the dead would be resurrected on the Day of Judgment here. Christian, Jewish and Muslim cemeteries thickly cover the valley. The tombs we want to photograph lie at the southern end. Barricades close the narrow road today. Neither of us feels like walking. Aram negotiates side streets and hills to find the perfect overlook.

Absalom's Tomb, probably the most impressive of the tombs, holds architectural interest. An inscription on the tomb states that it belongs to John the Baptist's father. Josephus mentions it in his historical writings. It dates back to the first century, the Second Temple period. This traditional site stimulates teaching and remembering. Absalom, King David's son tried to take his father's kingdom among other rebellious acts. He died when his mount ran under trees. Absalom's hair caught in the branches where he hanged until soldiers killed him. Fathers bring their sons here to throw rocks at the monument to demonstrate what happens to rebellious sons. The historical site of the monument Absalom erected to his own memory remains outside the city of Jerusalem.

II Samuel 18:18 provides some enlightenment on the historical significance of the tomb, *"During his lifetime Absalom had taken a pillar and erected it in the King's Valley as a monument to himself, for he thought, 'I have no son to carry on the memory of my name.'"* He named the pillar after himself, and it is called Absalom's Monument to this day. It really isn't his tomb, but a monument to himself. The monument remains empty, sort of like the life Absalom lived.

Archaeologists believe the Cave of Jehoshaphat, later added to Absalom's Pillar, accommodated the offspring of the families already buried here. It took its name from the location, the Valley of Jehoshaphat. Legend reports the cave serves as the burial place of King Jehoshaphat, but the Bible tells us King Jehoshaphat lies buried inside the City of David. I don't argue with Scripture. I patiently wait for future archaeological discoveries. A lintel in Jehoshaphat's Cave elaborately adorned with both Eastern and Hellenistic artistry intrigues the archaeologist in me, but I won't get to see it today.

Jerusalem Footsteps Through Time by Ahron Horovitz tells the story of the Tomb of Zechariah situated in the Hinnom Valley near Absalom's Tomb.

> *One of the most important tombs in Jewish tradition is the Tomb of Zechariah. Its vicinity was a resting place for the righteous throughout the generations. When the kings of Judah continued to worship idols, rousing God's wrath, a brave kohen [priest] admonished:*

> *"And the Spirit of God enveloped Zechariah, son of Jehoiada the priest, and he stood above the people and said to them: 'Thus said the Lord: Why do you transgress the command of God? You will not succeed, for you have abandoned God, and He has abandoned you.' The people plotted against him and stoned him at the command of the king, in the courtyard of the Temple (II Chronicles 24:20-21).*

> *This crime was especially serious, since it occurred in the Temple courtyard, and on a Yom Kippur coinciding with Shabbat. "The Jews committed seven sins that day: They killed a priest and a prophet, spilled innocent blood, defiled the azarah, and desecrated both Shabbat and Yom Kippur." (Jerusalem Talmud, Ta'anit 4:8).*

> *The Talmud relates that when the Babylonians burnt down the first Temple, the murdered prophet's blood began to boil. The Assyrian General Nebuzaradan asked what was going on:*

> *The children of Israel said to him "This is the blood of a priest and prophet who prophesied to Israel about the destruction of Jerusalem and was killed for it." He said to them, "I will appease him." He brought sages and killed them over [Zechariah's] blood. But the blood did not rest. He brought young apprentices of the priesthood and killed them, but the blood did not rest. He approached the blood and said, "Zechariah! Zechariah! I have disposed of the finest of your people; do you wish that I kill them all?" Immediately the blood stopped boiling. (Sanhedrin 96b)*

The legend of Zechariah's boiling blood deeply impressed generations to come. In the fourth century, Christian and, later, Arab visitors pointed out bloodstains of Zechariah on the Temple Mount. Rabbi Menachem Mendel of Kaminetz wrote in 1835, "Next to the Tomb of Zechariah stands a low dome, and on top is blood. Other places turn red when water is poured on them. [People] say this is the blood of the Jews Nebuzaradan slaughtered on account of Zechariah." Zechariah's Tomb became a symbol of the destruction of the first temple. Since the Middle Ages, Jews have come to this site to mourn on the 9th of Av. One Jewish traveler describes his experience in 1693:

And all the people of Jerusalem go there every year on the eve of the 9th of Av. They weep and cry profusely over the destruction of the Temple. And they lament the murder of Zechariah the prophet. After that, a Rabbi gives a sermon, and they read Lamentations and relate works that break the heart. [The Jews] sit there until midnight, when each man goes to the graves of his fathers – and the women to the Tomb of Zechariah – and from there to a nearby cave where Gedaliah, son of Ahikam, is buried.

Though Zechariah was killed by his brethren, later generations did not feel he would bear a grudge against them for the actions of their ancestors. These descendants even turned to him in prayer. During a drought in 1651, Moslem authorities pressured the Jews to pray for rain, threatening them if it didn't fall within three days. The Jews fasted and appealed to Zechariah:

"Though we have sinned and transgressed against you and killed you, we dare raise our heads to ask that you pray for us, for we know that you will have mercy on us and pray for us before God, and today it shall be known that there is a God in Israel."

Immediately, the people burst into tears – men, women, and children at the Tomb of Zechariah – until their crying reached Heaven. God changed His plan to punish them, and the sky darkened with clouds and wind.

Rabbi Samuel then sent a message to a minister of state, saying: 'Saddle [your horse], and go down, so you will not be delayed by the rain.'

"And the rain came down on the land, blessed and merciful rain, and it was a miracle" (Vilnai 254).

Although traditions going back to the fourth century identify this tomb as Zechariah's, its design suggests otherwise. The Ionic columns and capitals running along its four sides, and the Egyptian style cornice, led Professor Nachman Avigad to date the tomb to the end of the Second Temple period.

The structure may be the 'nefesh' – the monument signifying the soul's departure from the body and ascent to Heaven – of the nearby Bnei Hezir Tomb, since no grave was found inside it.

Despite the clash between the tradition and archeology, Zechariah's Tomb retains an important place in the Jewish peoples' memories.[50]

We thank *Jerusalem Footsteps Through Time* for enlightening us regarding the Tomb of Zechariah. Below Zechariah's Tomb lies the Tomb of Hezir's Sons. The rectangular opening has two Doric columns. An inscription referring to the "sons of Hezir," a Jewish priestly family, helped identify this tomb. I snap more pictures. Aram offers us a ride through the countryside to the ancient city of Jericho. Billed as the "oldest city in the world," I journeyed there in 1998 as part of my class. Even though we came to Jerusalem to spend time in the Old City, we consider going outside the city to Jericho.

Right now we ride through the Hinnom Valley, an infamous place known in ancient times as a dump and place of constant fires. The pagans sacrificed their own children to false gods here. King Josiah's actions regarding this place are recorded in 2 Kings 23:10, *"He [Josiah] desecrated Topeth, which was in the Valley of Ben Hinnom, so no one could use it to sacrifice his son or daughter in the fire to Molech."* Jeremiah wrote in 19:6, *"So beware, the days are coming, declares the Lord, when people will no longer call this place Topheth*

---

50 Reprinted from "Jerusalem Footsteps through Time" by Ahron Horovitz with permission from Feldheim Publishers.

or the valley of Ben Hinnom, but the valley of slaughter." Ben Hinnom means the sons of Hinnom. No one seems to know the history of those people. I'm guessing they owned the valley at one time.

This Hebrew name, transliterated into Greek becomes *gehenna*, the word for hell. While I was here in 1998, it snowed in the Hinnom Valley. I have in my possession a picture of hell frozen over from that day! Today, thick smoke rolls out of the tree covered valley floor. Aram assures us only trash burns. He takes us up the Mount of Olives to a quiet spot with a panoramic view of the Temple Mount. He avoids the tourist trap with the camel. I feel sadness come over me. We will soon leave Jerusalem. As our taxi maneuvers narrow streets we peer between Palestinian homes and buildings seeing the Judean desert in the distance. Aram stops at the Mount of Olives Chapel of Ascension (written in eight languages on the sign). It's a mosque. Why Muslims have a mosque to commemorate the ascension of Jesus mystifies me, but we know the answer. We shrug our shoulders and say, "Because this is Jerusalem!"

According to legend, a Christian noble woman built the first chapel here around 380AD. Somehow, the image of Christ's footprint miraculously appeared here on the Mount of Olives where Jesus ascended into Heaven. We enter the very small spherical room, perhaps 15 feet in diameter. A young family prays near the center of the mosque. The man lays prostrate toward the marble boxed footprint and lights candles on the floor in the sand. His wife reads from a holy book. I can't see the title. Three small children cling to her. We kneel and pray a short prayer. Then Aram lights two candles and hands each of us one. I stick mine in the sand. I lean toward the recessed stone in the marble box and press my fingertips on the imprint of the foot. I thank God for Christ's ascension into Heaven. Tears well up in my eyes, as I remember how the disciples must have felt to see Him go. He had to leave. While Jesus remained here on earth, He could only be in one place at a time. After His ascension, He sent the Holy Spirit. Now He lives with us all the time, wherever we go. God's ways are not our ways. Who can understand it? No one does, but we trust Him.

Aram turns toward the West Bank city of Jericho. We pass through the beautiful hills of Judea, giving way to wilderness. The wilderness gives way to the Judean desert. Stark, brown, dry, fluffy looking dunes rise to meet the sky again and again. On the new road to Jericho, I think of the old road to Jericho. The old gravel road allowed one to look deep into the Valley of the Shadow of Death and see St. George's Monastery, accessible only by donkey or on foot. Aram finds the old road. In poor condition, a huge cement barricade partially blocks the road. Aram stops and talks to some Bedouins. They tell him the closed road sign warns buses. Aram swerves to pass the red warning sign and continues down the forbidden road. The narrow road and blind corners make me close my eyes and tighten my seat belt. We come to a dangerous wash-out. Miraculously, Aram squeezes around it where no bus could. Finally, we arrive at the entrance to the lookout for the monastery. Here you decide to ride the donkey or walk. I point out the very narrow foot path three stories below to David. We opt to continue our journey to Jericho.

On the road to Jericho.

Bedouin tents along the way provide another example of the ancient inter-tangled with the present. Black tents huddle in the desert wilderness with satellite TV dishes set up nearby. Children play outside tents, boys ride donkeys, clothes hang out to dry, decorating the drab, sand colored hills. Goats run along the road. A lone camel stands in front of a Bedouin tent.

A red sign looms ahead:

Palestinian Authority Territory

Area Ahead

No Entry for Israelis

Entry Illegal by Israeli Law

We can't claim Israeli citizenship, but not because we wouldn't want to. Aram tells us the guards at the checkpoint may ask for ID. I panic. My passport sits securely in the hotel safe. When I left this morning, I had no idea I would be going to the West Bank city of Jericho. David informs Aram he carries copies of our passports with him. Aram thinks everything is all right. I can't help but focus on the big guns hanging across the soldiers' chests. Aram says a few words in Arabic. One of the guards yells at David, "What is your name?" David answers and the guard smiles and waves us through. Aram roars through the checkpoint and takes us on a taxi tour of Jericho. We pass fruit stands, farmers' markets, clothing shops, apartments, homes, and points of interest, all narrated by Aram. There are lots of palm trees in Jericho. In the Book Deuteronomy 34:3, *"...the Valley of Jericho, the City of Palms...,"* Moses describes the land God is giving to the descendants of Abraham, Isaac, and Jacob. At over 840 feet below sea level, Jericho feels hotter than the Hinnom Valley, if you get my drift!

Our interest lies in the ancient Tel, northwest of the modern city. Aram tries to talk us into taking the cable car up to the Monastery of Temptation. My recent experience with heights (the ramparts) convinces me not to include cable cars in this tour. We opt to climb Tel Jericho (also known as Tel es-Sultan). In this heat we advance slowly to the top. I show David the excavations my class explored in 1998. We behold ancient Jericho, one of the oldest fortified cities in the world. Archaeologists consider this tower, constructed by what they call *stone- age* people, a supreme achievement. A Canaanite city wall from 2000 BC, along with city gates from 1500 BC, reveals wonders of past civilizations. Tels have civilizations built on top of each other, making excavation difficult. Deciding which level to expose creates challenges. What treasures lie just beneath the level chosen haunts archaeologists.

Aram says for us to take our time. He will wait. We spend over an hour on the Tel. At around 110 degrees, I believe the heat works to our advantage. No one else tours the Tel at the time. A couple of times I need to sit under the grass-covered awning, getting some relief from the sun. Being up here alone feels fantastic. I hum the old Sunday school song, *"Joshua fought the battle of Jericho, Jericho, Jericho. And the walls came tumblin' down."*

When we get down the Tel, Aram offers to take us anywhere. Do we want to go to the Dead Sea? Masada? Qumran? No. No. No. We have done plenty for one day. We want to go back to the Gloria before dark. Aram drives us back via the Mount of Olives. Coming down the front side, we find ourselves on a road slightly larger than the width of our taxi with ten-foot walls on each side. Aram doesn't slow down. The winding road lends little visibility on the sharp curves. I fear for our lives and the lives of whomever might become a hood ornament. Aram, an excellent driver, leans on the horn most of the way. A young female pedestrian pokes her head around the corner just in time to jump back against the wall as we flash by. Whoa! We meet an oncoming taxi, followed by another car. They refuse to retreat. Unbelievable! More than a mile into this topless tunnel, we have only a quarter of a mile to go. Aram stands firm. My mouth drops open when the other driver inches forward to a slight bulge in the stone wall. The other car follows. You can't get your pinkie finger between our taxi and their vehicles as we creep by. It's Jerusalem!

Aram lets us out at Jaffa Gate. We stop to buy bread. The man wants to charge me ten shekels apiece. Yesterday I paid seven shekels. I start to argue, but the other fellow says "all right," and I pay seven shekels each. I am happy. Later, David's bread is good, but mine is stale and hard. The fellow sold me one loaf of day old bread. The price wasn't such a good deal after all. You get what you pay for!

THE TWENTY-FIFTH DAY

"Peter replied, 'Repent and be baptized, every one of you, in the name of Jesus Christ for the forgiveness of your sins. And you will receive the gift of the Holy Spirit'" (Acts 2:38).

Christ Church celebrates the Day of Pentecost this beautiful morning. People say Jerusalem's weather is like California. That might account for

Issa reads the Lord's Prayer in Aramaic.

the tarantulas! On the way to Christ Church, a voice calls out, "Hey, you guys!" We turn to see Issa from Murad's shop in the Christian Quarter. It feels homey having a friend stop us to chat. The conversation leads to how much it costs to live in Jerusalem. Issa wants to buy a taxi because of slow business at the shop. The shop supports five families. Five families require more money than the shop generates. Issa used to drive a tour bus, so he knows his way around. Three weeks ago, he told me his name means Jesus in Aramaic. He read the Lord's Prayer to us in Aramaic. I remember that as a special moment. After a short visit, we continue our hike to Christ Church.

Pentecost, the day Christians celebrate receiving the gift of the Holy Spirit, coincides with the Jewish holiday of Shavuot. Shavuot celebrates God giving the Ten Commandments to the Hebrews. He wrote the Ten Commandments on stone fifty days after the destroyer of the first-born passed over the children of Israel, delivering them from destruction. The story of Pentecost begins at Christ's resurrection. Fifty days after His resurrection, the disciples received the Holy Spirit. As promised in Jeremiah 31:31-33, God wrote His laws on their hearts. Just before Christ's ascension he opened the minds of the disciples so they could understand the Scriptures. At that time, the New Testament did not yet exist. Therefore, Jesus spoke of the Old Testament and the Prophets. He explained to the disciples that the Scriptures foretold he would suffer and die. On the third day he would rise from the dead. These things had already been witnessed by the disciples.

Now he told them that repentance and forgiveness of sins would be preached in His name throughout the world beginning at Jerusalem. They would also witness this. In addition, He would send the Holy Spirit. They were to stay in Jerusalem until they received the Holy Spirit. They stayed near the Temple in Jerusalem praising God and waiting for the next ten days, adding up to fifty days since the resurrection. In an upper room near the Temple a supernatural event instantly changed their lives.

A violent rushing wind filled the place and they saw tongues of fire that came to rest on each one of the disciples. At that moment, they were filled with the Holy Spirit and began to speak in languages they had not previously known. Jews from all parts of the world were gathered in Jerusalem at the time to celebrate Shavuot! Peter and the disciples began preaching in these languages. About three thousand people repented and were saved that day. This story of Pentecost related in Acts, chapter two, marks the receiving of the Holy Spirit. The Holy Spirit changed the disciples from weak, tired, frightened individuals to men of power filled with purpose. When we receive Christ, we receive the Holy Spirit. Jesus called the Holy Spirit the Comforter. Galatians 5:22-23 reveals the fruit of the Holy Spirit as love, joy, peace, patience, kindness, goodness, faithfulness, gentleness, and self control.

I expect this morning's sermon to focus on Peter on that first day of Pentecost. Instead, Pastor David Pileggi gives another appropriate message. I like the way he preaches, low key, honest, transparent. The message speaks of how we all want to get to Heaven. We all want to live with God. "But," the pastor says, "God wants to come here." Wow. It's an interesting concept and so true. God wants righteousness and obedience here on earth so He can come and live among us. I admire the creativity and truth in the message. After the message, we are blessed to take part in Holy Communion with strangers in the flesh and family in the Spirit.

During the service, a man gives his testimony about how he went to the hospital last week because of a heart attack. The doctors fixed a blockage in a major artery. He testifies to having no fear during the attack, surgery, or the three days recovering in intensive care. He looks familiar. I whisper to David, "Isn't he the man from Falafel Chapel?"

"He brought us juice at Murad's shop," David remembers. After church, the pastor invites people to stay for refreshments and fellowship. The falafel man serves orange juice.

When he hands me my drink he surprises me saying, "Do you remember me?" Of course we remember him, but after all the customers he sees every day, we respond with delight that he remembers us. We find a shady table. A man from Bethlehem, named Issa, joins us. Another Issa! This Issa preaches at a Bethlehem church. He talks about Bethlehem and all the changes that happened since we visited in 1999. "Bethlehem once had a Christian population of 70%, but now only 30% because of all the unrest." We chat about the 2002 occupation of the Church of the Nativity by Hamas and PLO terrorists. Issa lives near the Church of the Nativity. For thirty days, a blockade isolated him and his family. They could get no food or supplies. They crawled and lay on the floor for fear of bullets coming in the windows. An Israeli tank ran into a light pole and they lost power. Issa thanks God that neither him nor any of his family suffered injuries during this difficult time.

Issa tells us his church offers a Bed and Breakfast. It's much cheaper to stay there, in Bethlehem, than in Jerusalem. One of the elders of Christ Church, Dave, joins our table. Dave helped serve communion earlier. Dave stayed at Issa's Bed and Breakfast. He reveals it is on a very steep street. Issa says, "It's five minutes from the Church of the Nativity."

Dave quips, "If you had a skateboard, it would be five seconds." My little dream cloud forming about returning to Israel for six months at Issa's Bed and Breakfast in Bethlehem vanished!

Dave shares of his upcoming marriage, on the 27th of the next month. His fiancé joins us. He lived in Canada. She came from Australia. They met here and plan on living in Jerusalem. We visit with them a little while, wish them well, and return to the Gloria.

Back at the Gloria, David decides to visit some museums I saw in 1998. It will be a good opportunity for me to write. Later I go to the modern mall looking for some blouses or a dress for Cynthia's wedding. Should I wear Middle Eastern embroidery at an American wedding? I'm just not quite there on either of them. All three of us sisters still haven't decided what we're planning to wear that day. The modern mall disappoints. Back at the Gloria, I write, rest, do some emails, and think about packing for our return flight. David returns, reporting his adventures in the Jewish Quarter.

First of all he visits the Wohl Museum – the Herodian Quarter. After 1967, when Israel started rebuilding the Jewish Quarter, archaeologists found several Herodian houses destroyed in 70AD. These homes of the wealthy priestly class contain their own mikvahs. Intact Jewish mosaic floors and walls remain. Modern society learns a lot about the priestly class from these houses and Burnt House, which he visits next. Archaeologists found Burnt House first. A Roman spear embedded in a woman led to speculation about a back story. A movie dramatizes the story of the family who once lived in that house. They actually know the name of the family from some finds here. The movie portrays the division between the Zealots, the Priests, and the common class.

If the Zealots had not burned the storehouses, Jerusalem would have held out much longer. Hungry people started resenting the daily sacrifices. The Zealots hated Roman oppression. They stood up to Rome in rebellion for four years. People thought the Temple would never be destroyed. Sadly, history reveals their error. Jewish sages admit God had Titus destroy Jerusalem and the Temple in 70AD because of "needless, underserved hatred between Jews." God expects love, understanding, and unity among His people. The Bible records God protecting Jerusalem in the past against armies as terrifying as the Romans. In 70AD, He allowed the consequences of their rebellion against His ways.

Next, David visits the Temple Institute. Implements made for the Third Temple stand on display. Guards with guns prohibit picture taking in any of these museums. This rule frustrates David. Kids with their teachers and bodyguards tour the Wohl Museum and the Temple Institute. The kids cross ropes, touch walls, and play with delicate models. It's hard to imagine how pictures could hurt more than kids touching, but – this is Jerusalem!

Upon David's return, we begin packing. We break for dinner and go upstairs to find the dining room closed. A note on the door apologizes. They hope the relocation of the dining room won't cause any inconvenience. The reception desk tells us tonight the Knight's Palace, their other hotel, serves dinner. It's only five minutes up the hill, of course. We dine on Shawarmas and sodas at a little hole in the wall, one minute away. This covered street made into a couple of places to eat, intrigues David. It's different. David insists Craig came here back in 1998 with his college buddies. He calls it "Craig's Cave." I doubt Craig even knows it exists.

We relax and people-watch, enjoying our last Jerusalem sunset. We had better finish packing. Tomorrow we have to check out by 10 a.m. David packs with determination and expertise. Everything finally fits in the bags but they weigh too much. When we left Denver, they met the 50-pound limit. Now they weigh more. He may have to pack our books in a second carry on. We stop worrying about it and decide to do what we have to at check-in. Finally we sleep. Our last night at the Gloria Hotel in the Old City of Jerusalem seems surreal. Didn't we just arrive yesterday? How could it possibly be time to leave?

The Twenty-Sixth Day

Yad Vashem

"…to them I will give within my temple and its walls a memorial and a name better than sons and daughters; I will give them an everlasting name that will not be cut off" (Isaiah 56:5).

This morning we finish packing and go upstairs to the dining room. The weird breakfast buffet I hated twenty-six days ago looks good. I have come to love the grain cereal with yogurt and honey. The coffee tastes delicious. I thoroughly enjoy breakfast. We pick up our laundry. I'm going to miss all the service and attention here at the Gloria. Upon checking out, the manager graciously offers to let use a room sometime during the day to rest if we need it. He knows our flight doesn't leave until midnight. We store our luggage in the Gloria office. The office books us a sherut to get us to Tel Aviv and Ben Gurion International Airport. A 6:00 p.m. departure might work, but with rush hour I thought we should leave at 5:00 p.m. instead. The manager insists on 4:00 p.m. We book a 4:00 p.m. ride to the airport for our 11:35 p.m. flight. It's Jerusalem.

One thing we know we must do before we leave Jerusalem. Neither of us has been to Yad Vashem, the holocaust museum. Perhaps we should have gone sooner, but today we feel sad as our dream trip draws to an end. Our somber mood makes today the right time to visit. We go to the taxi stand at Jaffa Gate. They recognize us. One driver remembers taking us to our friend's home for Shabbat. It's a small world at the Jaffa Gate taxi stand.

Yad Vashem looms larger than either one of us imagined. At the cloakroom, we check David's small backpack (required) and get recommended cane-stools on loan. These contraptions make nice chairs, but horrible canes. They will help us get through this enormous museum. Upon entering the concrete vault, Yad Vashem Museum, a sign warns us that we enter a lost world. Many short film clips appear in a moving map showing glimpses of pre-Hitler Jewish life in those countries. Some scenes look cold and snowy, others, sunny and warmer. Music, skating, singing,

Torah study, and lots of Jewish dancing fill the screens. Watching these happy people and knowing how their lives change dramatically wrenches my heart.

Endless exhibits contain testimonies of events affecting this or that family. A film on Christian anti-Semitism forces me to muster my resolve to watch. Every fiber of my being wants to deny the Christian Churches' anti-Semitism portrayed in the movie. I catch a glimpse of how logical people could deny the holocaust. People claim it never occurred when their mind cannot accept facts as truth. The portrayal of anti-Semitic Christians feels so contrary to my experience. My mind rebels and I want to move on. My brain keeps rejecting the facts presented, even though the well-documented film contains original footage, shots of cartoons slamming Jews, and position papers of the church. We both grieve in revulsion and disgust at the inhumane treatment of the Jews by Christians.

We agree the museum protects important facts. Without proof, the mind cannot accept the idea that Christians or Germans could behave the way they did. Several telling exhibits portray how German society integrated the Jews. Jews could not believe what happened. One year they serve with honor in the military. The next year they get thrown out of the military as undesirables. In a couple more years they become hunted down by the military and sent to death camps. Societal values changed so quickly. The end times will be like that for all believers.

We tried our best to skip through the death camp scenes. David and I had seen enough in the liberation movies we watched before we came. One scene of a skeleton man, naked, walking around – just bones and flesh – no meat at all, horrified me and indelibly emblazons a place in my brain. I wish I could forget that scene. I cannot imagine the inhumanity forcing that man to such a wretched state. I could not believe he was up and walking as the camp was liberated. We rest and recoup a while, then eat lunch quietly. Sadness weighs us down. Chatting seems irreverent.

On the path to the exit we pass a hillside, home to over 20 monuments for six million Jews. Beyond that we view the Jerusalem forest, where trees have been planted in memory of the dead. Again, words cannot express our sorrow and grief for these innocent victims. It is quiet.

Yad Vashem monument.

We hail a taxi back to Jaffa Gate. We hit Craig's cave for refreshment. Watching the action at Jaffa Square, we slowly come out of our funk. Jerusalem has been an extraordinary experience.

The sherut ride to the airport presents another tour for us. The empty van has two double seats, two single seats, and a four-person bench across the back. We take the front seats until we have to sit together. The big heavy blue backpack will soon have to ride on our laps, but for now it gets a seat. The driver must pick up eight Orthodox Jewish men scattered around Jerusalem before heading to the airport.

We ride through various Orthodox neighborhoods in Jerusalem just after schools let out. Kids play outside in the afternoon sun. It's fun to see families playing, shopping, picking up the mail, and so forth. A boy with his arm in a cast plays just as hard as his friends. Kids act the same everywhere no matter how they dress. Families behave the same too. Wives and kids come out to the van seeing their husbands and fathers off. Good-bye waves follow the van. One lucky guy gets a little kiss good-bye. We stop for the tenth passenger. David moves over and sits with me. The Orthodox man gets a nice surprise of a single seat.

Our driver seems impatient by Jerusalem's standards, but not by NYC standards. He honks a lot and almost leaves the father of two junior high kids behind. He may not like Orthodox Jews. Fortunately, another Orthodox Jew watches out and asks the kids in Hebrew how many? Two or three? The kids say three. When the driver takes off, the man yells for him to wait for the other passenger. The fact one passenger watches someone else's back makes me think prejudice against Orthodox Jews exists in Jerusalem. The driver listens to a Hebrew, not Arabic, radio station. Perhaps he, like so many in Jerusalem, rejects his Jewish faith. Perhaps he is just having a bad day.

We pick up passengers in Romma, Makor Baruch, Zucrihon Moshe, and Lerem Avraham. We go through lots of corners and back streets. The driver knows his way around these Orthodox neighborhoods. David asks the man who takes the seat he opened up to show him his house on our map. He man willingly obliges. Another answers his cell phone in Hebrew, then switches to English for the conversation, except when he would say, "Praise the Lord." Then he would say, "Baruch Hashem," in Hebrew. I smile because in any language God is great and is greatly to be praised. Someday very soon every knee will bow and every tongue will confess He is Lord. Baruch Hashem!

Soon we arrive at Ben Gurion International Airport. We lift off Israeli soil and leave Israeli airspace. I leave infected with Israel like so many pilgrims before me. Previous visits did not immunize me, instead they made me more susceptible. My mind, body, and spirit remain invaded by Israel. Already I contemplate my return.

FINAL THOUGHTS

"It is the glory of God to conceal a matter; to search out a matter is the glory of kings" (Proverbs 25:2).

In 2003, at a Biblical Counseling Conference in Colorado, Dr. Randall Price signed his book, *The Stones Cry Out,* for me. On the title page he wrote, "Dr. Vicki, Pursue the past." Beneath his signature he penned "Proverbs 25:2." This verse, written by Solomon, confirms that God receives glory even when men do not understand the universe and the way God designed life to work. A king rules well by discovering the truth, unearthing the mysteries and educating the masses. This goal remains the obsession of Biblical archaeology.

Jerusalem's archaeological finds intoxicated us. We get excited by things that confirm the Bible and force us to view the Bible as historical. I call this the stones crying out. We had stones call out to us in many ways. Standing stones remain as testimony to places and events that happened. The building Herod built still stands over Abraham's tomb. Although Hebron changed hands many times, these stones mark and protect the correct cave. Often ancient churches exhibit a tile floor or something through Plexiglas inset in the modern floor. The old floor stands as a stone testimony to the fact that the church remained in that same place over centuries.

The Church of All Nations construction began in 1920, relatively a young church for Jerusalem, but with deep historic significance. When construction began, fragments of an ancient mosaic were found, thus delaying construction. Excavation revealed a Crusader chapel, uninhabited since 1345, and underneath that, a fourth century Byzantine basilica destroyed by the 746AD earthquake that ravaged Jerusalem. The Church of All Nations houses the Rock of Agony said to be the rock Jesus leaned on when he prayed on the night of His crucifixion. I believe the rock could be *the* rock Jesus leaned on, but there is no mention of it being in the previous structures. Even though the Mount of Olives is a big place, you can see that for many, many centuries, this particular place has been identified as the place Jesus went aside from the twelve disciples to pray and sweat drops of blood.

For big events, I believe the traditional location is correct. A hundred years after John F. Kennedy's assassination, it will be easy to find someone in Dallas who can point out the Texas Book Depository and the grassy knoll. It might be harder to find the right hospital room or operating room because they are not important to the average citizen. Their location won't be passed from generation to generation. Locations of big events, like the spot of the crucifixion, the tomb, the betrayal with a kiss, would have been still known at the time Constantine's mother made her investigations. Mount Sinai, perhaps not so much. Unfortunately, no continuous presence kept track of Mount Sinai. When the cloud moved, they moved. Lazarus' tomb, although less important than God's gift of the law, had a continuous witness.

The Chapel of Ascension is traditional, not historical, in my mind. It depends on if the footprint occurred. Since the Bible doesn't mention a footprint, this may not be the exact spot. Still, this footprint spot has been used for generations as a standing stone to commemorate Jesus' ascension. The ascension did occur and it occurred near there. That rock witnessed the rising into the air, even if it is not the actual place where Jesus' foot last touched earth.

There is a reason God has not revealed exact locations of many significant events in the Bible. We must focus on our Creator instead of the creation. People might worship the site instead of God. Righteous King Hezekiah destroyed Moses' bronze snake because the Israelites had begun worshipping it (2 Kings 18:4). For us, the historical sites enhanced our worship of our God! In the Torah, God does not reveal the location of Moses' burial. Jews believe that God did not want them to know the location of Moses' burial because He did not want them to worship the man, thereby attaching any divinity to him.

There are a lot of people who smoke in Jerusalem. You are never really free of it. Even inside, where you are not supposed to smoke, it sneaks in and becomes an undertone everywhere. In 1998, I saw more smokers and smoking was permitted almost everywhere. Thankfully, now smoking is prohibited in many places. In restaurants, you may not be next to a smoker inside, but you almost certainly will be if you eat on a patio. Sadly, kids smoke, too. I mention this only because every smoker I know wants to quit.

There are so many kinds of people living together in Jerusalem. They work together pretty well. Especially now, that a generation or two have passed since 1967. However, tension and prejudice arise, too. Like everywhere else, people think the government takes too much in taxes and does too little for their particular group. The constant possibility that things could turn ugly at any moment keeps you more aware of your surroundings. Jews remember 1948, when neighbor started killing neighbor.

Armed guards go on every school field trip. Constant readiness for possible trouble shows up everywhere. That wears on you, but day to day there really is no danger. Kids act like all kids and play the same. They laugh and cry and have fun and eat ice cream. They love their parents at one age and ignore them at another. Some love God, while others don't care. It's the same everywhere. I hoped Jerusalem would be different, but it wasn't in Bible times and it isn't that different now.

Remember how there were three main languages in Jerusalem at the time of the crucifixion? "King of the Jews" was written in Aramaic, Greek, and Latin on the cross. Well, it's the same now. Most signs are written in three languages, English, Hebrew and Arabic. Jerusalem remains a three language city.

Jerusalem has crazy traffic. The traffic culture is different. In some ways drivers are more patient than those in NYC or downtown Denver. In Jerusalem, leaving half a car length between you and the next car upsets everyone. Even at red lights, drivers must move up every possible inch at every possible moment. No gaps, ever. On the other hand, drivers use hand signals to tell other cars, "I will let you in," or "Wait!" They take turns well. Lanes don't matter much either. They ebb and flow with the situation. If a truck is parked half on the sidewalk and half in a lane, the lanes just flow outward around it, the lines don't matter. Jerusalem's drivers have a culture that works. It is completely different from the US driving culture. I cannot imagine an American driving very well in the area around the Old City where the streets change their rules depending on the time of day, holiday status, or who is visiting Jerusalem.

Everyone who works for a living agrees that Jerusalem is a hard place to live. It is a difficult place to make enough income to get by. I never met any real white collar workers. I don't know how life is for them. Israel continues building a lot of nice new apartments for someone in both east and west Jerusalem suburbs. There must be a lot of people with money. They don't serve pizza, drive taxis, etc. Gas and food are very expensive; probably double what they cost here. Housing is perhaps double, too. It makes things tough. Even the public bus is six shekels ($1.50). Unlike our Colorado RTD, Jerusalem buses are well used and get lots of riders. Most cab rides cost $8 - $15, so they are similar to Manhattan.

I know the adventure we shared in Jerusalem opened spiritual doors for both of us. One of the biggest effects is the broadening of places we feel comfortable worshiping God. We prayed in the Church of the Holy Sepulcher and experienced the supernatural presence of God. We prayed in synagogues on Shavuot and felt the spirit of the Living God. We prayed silently on the Temple Mount, by the Dome of the Rock under a shade tree. We prayed in the Mosque of Ascension, experiencing God, acknowledging His ascension. We prayed at the Western Wall often. We prayed in the Churches we attended and the churches we toured.

Of all of these, the Church of the Holy Sepulcher was the strongest experience, which surprised David. Over the years, God slowly removed anti-Catholic prejudices in him. I think this trip finished it off. He had no trouble taking those cards for Mike's kids into the Church of the Holy Sepulcher, laying them on the Unction Stone, and praying over them.

My previous visits to the Church of the Holy Sepulcher turned me off because of the expensive ornate objects filling the church. I felt these articles took away from worship. Before, I focused on the fact that the Church of the Holy Sepulcher remained a "traditional site." I never prayed there before. I never knelt anywhere inside the church. Since then, I am convinced the Church of the Holy Sepulcher is indeed the historical site. Even more surprising to me is that I really don't care. It doesn't matter whether it is historical. God surrounds me. The fact that He blessed me with an incredible revelation in the Church of the Holy Sepulcher makes it special to me. If it had happened at the top of Mt. Nebo, it would have made Mt. Nebo special to me.

Our experience at King of Kings Church included Hebraic roots with traditional praise songs familiar to us. We especially enjoyed the Healing Pools. People reached out to us there and made us feel welcome. For regular church services, we liked Christ Church best. It combines a strong Protestant message with Hebrew roots understanding. So while the boundaries of where we can worship comfortably have expanded, the center remains the same.

The emphasis on holiness by many people in Jerusalem challenges me in that area. God may be dealing with me there next. He isn't finished with me yet and I look forward to how He will work in my life now. Baruch Hashem!

RECOMMENDED READING

Bennett, Arthur. Editor. *The Valley of Vision*
The Banner of Truth Trust, 2002.

Blech, Rabbi Benjamin *The Complete Idiot's Guide to Jewish History and Culture*
The Penguin Group, 2004.

Eisenberg, Ronald L. *Streets of Jerusalem*
Devora Publishing Company, 2006.

Eisenberg, Ronald L. *The 613 Mitzvot*
Schreiber Publishing, 2005.

Garrard, Alec *The Splendor of the Temple*
Kregel Publications, 2000.

Heschel, Abraham Joshua *The Sabbath*
Farrar, Straus, and Giroux, 1951.

Horovitz, Ahron. *Jerusalem Footsteps Through Time*
Feldeim Publishers, 2000, 2001.

Kolatch, Alfred J. *The Jewish Book of Why*
The Penguin Group, 2000.

Kollek, Teddy. *My Jerusalem*
Summit Books, 1990.

Murphy-O'Connor, Jerome. *The Holy Land*
Oxford Press, 1998.

Price, Randall. *The Stones Cry Out*
Harvest House Publishers, 1997.

Ritmeyer, Leen and Kathleen *Jerusalem in the Year 30 A.D.*
Carta, Jerusalem, 2004.

Schoen, Robert. *What I Wish My Christian Friends Knew about Judaism*
Loyola Press, 2004.

Stern, David H. Complete Jewish Bible
Jewish New Testament Publications, 1998.

Wilson, Marvin R. *Our Father Abraham*
Wm. B. Eerdmans Publishing Company and
Center for Judaic-Christian Studies, 1989.

Young, Brad H. *Jesus the Jewish Theologian*
Hendrickson Publishers, Inc., 1995.

INDEX

CPSIA information can be obtained at www.ICGtesting.com
227160LV00006B/84/P

9 781593 306335